The Poacher from Stratford

Mr. WILLIAM

SHAKESPEARES

COMEDIES,
HISTORIES, &
TRAGEDIES.

Published according to the True Originall Copies.

L.O N D O N
Printed by Isaac Iaggard, and Ed. Blount. 1623.

The Droeshout Portrait of Shakespeare,
from the 1623 Folio

The Poacher from Stratford

A PARTIAL ACCOUNT OF THE CONTROVERSY OVER THE AUTHORSHIP OF SHAKESPEARE'S PLAYS

by

Frank W. Wadsworth

UNIVERSITY OF CALIFORNIA PRESS

Berkeley and Los Angeles

1958

University of California Press
Berkeley and Los Angeles, California
Cambridge University Press
London, England
© *1958 by The Regents of the University of California*
Library of Congress Catalog Card No.: 58-12094
Published in the United States of America
Designed by John B. Goetz

To
R. N. W.
who knows who wrote this.

ACKNOWLEDGMENTS

In writing this book I have been aided by more people than can be listed here. To all of them, I want to express my sincere thanks. To Messrs. W & A Gilbey and to John J. Espey, for whom thanks is hardly enough, I owe a greater debt; they are responsible for whatever virtues this account may possess (but are by no means to be blamed for its faults).

Acknowledgment is also due the following for their permission to print copyright material: Dodd, Mead and Company for a passage from G. G. Greenwood, *The Shakespeare Problem Restated;* the Francis Bacon Foundation for passages from *The Burial of Francis Bacon and His Mother in the Lichfield Chapter House;* William Maclellan Publishers, Ltd., for passages from W. J. Fraser Hutcheson, *Shakespeare's Other Anne;* George Elliott Sweet for passages from *Shake-speare The Mystery;* the United Press for photographs of the opening of Sir Thomas Walsingham's tomb.

CONTENTS

ILLUSTRATIONS

Frontispiece

The Droeshout Portrait of Shakespeare, from the 1623 Folio

Following page 18

Portrait of Mrs. Constance Pott, from Ignatius Donnelly,
The Great Cryptogram

Facsimile of page of 1623 Folio used by Ignatius Donnelly
as a worksheet, from *The Great Cryptogram*

Photograph of Dr. Orville W. Owen's WHEEL, from
Sir Francis Bacon's Cipher Story

Title page, "Gustavi Seleni Cryptomenytices et Cryptographiae," from Sir Edwin Durning-Lawrence,
Bacon Is Shake-speare

PROLOGUE

Among the books published in recent years was one by a
Mr. George Elliott Sweet of Malibu Beach, California. Entitled *Shake-speare The Mystery* and attractively printed,
the volume presents the interesting theory that the plays
and poems commonly ascribed to the pen of William
Shakespeare were actually the work of Elizabeth Tudor,
Queen of England from 1558 to 1603. According to Mr.
Sweet, Elizabeth made three vows: the first, to celibacy, at
the age of fifteen; the second, of marriage to England,
when she ascended the throne at twenty-five; the third, to
literature, when she realized at the age of forty-five that
"the children of her marriage to England would have to
be literary children." The result of this last promise was the
so-called Shakespearean writings, palmed off upon an un-
suspecting Elizabethan society as the work of a Stratford
actor chosen for the sensible reason that his name expressed
the Queen's political philosophy of "talk softly and carry a
big stick." The secret remained inviolate, unsuspected by

literary historians, until revealed at last by the light of Mr. Sweet's "scientific approach."

The reader of *Shake-speare The Mystery* hardly needs to be told that George Elliott Sweet is not alone in denying that William Shakespeare of Stratford wrote the works bearing his name. Within the past few years a gentleman from Long Island has opened an ancient Kentish tomb in an effort to prove that Christopher Marlowe was the actual author; an American newspaper has run a series of articles in favor of Sir Francis Bacon; and a group of eminent sceptics have inserted a paid advertisement in *The Shake-speare Newsletter* to the effect that Edward de Vere, seventeenth Earl of Oxford, was the true father of the plays. Yet the reader might find it helpful in deciding just what to do with Mr. Sweet and his theory to be reminded that behind them both lies a long and enlightening history of literary research based on the belief that Shakespeare could not have written the plays himself; just as he might find it significant to know (as Mr. Sweet, apparently, does not) that the thesis of *Shake-speare The Mystery* was accurately predicted some forty-five years ago by the prominent Shakespeare scholar, Mr. J. M. Robertson.

Like Mr. Sweet, most people who are convinced that Shakespeare was an imposter make certain assumptions. One is that Shakespeare was an obscure man about whom suspiciously little information has survived. Had his really been the genius responsible for the plays, contemporary documents would be rich in references to William Shakespeare, all praising him ecstatically as a second Homer or Vergil. Behind this belief is the hypothetical picture of an Elizabethan London with many of the features of the literary capital of Browning's day, a city of poetry societies presided over by venerable ladies and gentlemen, of literary teas sparked by lively discussions of the techniques of Shakespeare's art. In the absence of any evidence that such

Victorian appreciation was ever accorded the man from Stratford, it becomes necessary, we are informed, to conclude that he did not write the plays. Yet the truth is that Shakespeare was rather frequently mentioned by his fellow writers, particularly when one considers his status as an actor and popular dramatist; and Francis Meres, if he did not liken him to Homer or Vergil, did compare him favorably to Ovid and Plautus and Seneca.

Thus the complaint of many admirers of the Bard that they find our knowledge of his life disappointingly small comes as some surprise to the literary historian, who is himself more inclined to marvel that we know as much about Shakespeare as we do. Actually, the records of his life are not as meager as is frequently assumed. Between April 26, 1564, when his baptism was noted in the parish register at Stratford-on-Avon, and April 25, 1616, when the register recorded his burial within the same church, his name appears in connection with more than forty pieces of valid historical evidence (this count ignores the many records concerned with his parents, children, and grandchildren). These references provide an amount of biographical detail at least equal to that available for most of Shakespeare's fellow dramatists; far greater than the few facts surviving about such Elizabethan writers as John Webster and Cyril Tourneur. When one considers that there were no newspapers (at least in the modern sense of the word) in Shakespeare's day, and that few documents were consciously and systematically preserved for posterity, it seems astonishing that we have as much information as we do. Shakespeare and his fellow dramatists were workaday members of a workaday world—they had little contact with serious affairs of state; and actors, when invited to court, came to provide entertainment, not instruction. As a large part of today's knowledge of that period of history comes from state records, court diaries, and intelligencers' letters (politically oriented reports by the extensive if loosely organized Elizabethan secret service), it is small wonder that the doings of theatrical men do not loom large on the Elizabethan scene as historians reconstruct it.

In a similar manner—and for somewhat similar reasons —modern knowledge of the provenance of Elizabethan dramatic literature is neither extensive nor detailed. There was, in Shakespeare's day, no such thing as our copyright law. A dramatist was commissioned to write a play; when he had finished it and received his fee, the play was no longer his but the actors'. Production achieved, they could if they wished publish it, in which case a copy may well have survived into the twentieth century. Or they could put it away in whatever form of theatrical library they had— perhaps an actor's trunk or a disused writing stand. In either event, the manuscript was soon forgotten, and probably soon lost, for the actors were not unduly solicitous of posterity, and only Ben Jonson among Shakespeare's contemporaries seems to have had any real interest in the fate of his plays once they had served their day upon the boards. It is discouraging to speculate on what ignoble end the average Elizabethan dramatic manuscript must have come to; one good-sized batch, it is now known, perished as paper for the baking of pies. Thus one should not be surprised that few plays from the Elizabethan professional theater have survived in manuscript, or that Shakespeare's plays, like those of most of his fellow dramatists, have come down to us by means of early editions alone. And these editions, it might be noted by way of postscript, are far from being accurate or dependable, containing not only countless printing errors and frequent prompt-copy contaminations, but all the vagaries of the irregular Elizabethan spelling as well.

Sixteen of Shakespeare's plays appeared during his lifetime in such editions. These quartos, as they are usually known, represent varying degrees of textual accuracy, some of them, the so-called bad or pirated quartos (i.e., unauthorized by either the actors or their official publishers), being almost unreadable in places. Although the earliest plays were issued anonymously, Shakespeare's name appears on title pages from 1598 on with increasing frequency and in such a way as to indicate a growing popular appeal. Earlier his two long poems, *Venus and Adonis* and *The Rape of Lucrece,* had been published, in 1593 and 1594 respectively, with dedications to the Earl of Southampton by "William Shakespeare." In 1609 *Shake-speares Sonnets* were brought out in quarto.

A rather different publishing venture was the folio collection of 1623, made by Shakespeare's actor-colleagues, John Heminge and Henry Condell, seven years after the dramatist's death. Containing all the plays now held to comprise the Shakespeare canon, with the exception of *Pericles,* the First Folio was an act of friendship designed to give the reading public true and readable texts.

It had bene a thing, we confesse, worthie to have bene wished, that the Author himselfe had liv'd to have set forth, and overseen his owne writings; But since it hath bin ordain'd otherwise, and he by death departed from that right, we pray you do not envie his Friends, the office of their care, and paine, to have collected & publish'd them; and so to have publish'd them, as where (before) you were abus'd with diverse stolne, and surreptitious copies, maimed, and deformed by the frauds and stealthes of injurious imposters, that expos'd them: even those, are now offer'd to your view cur'd, and perfect of their limbes; and all the rest, absolute in their numbers, as he conceived them.

The Folio contains an engraving of Shakespeare which, according to Ben Jonson's lines to the reader on the opposite page, "was for gentle Shakespeare cut," and various commendatory verses, including Jonson's famous poem describing Shakespeare as "not of an age, but for all time!"

But perhaps the most moving panegyric in the volume is that of the actor-editors with whom Shakespeare's life had been so long and so closely associated. In "The Epistle Dedicatorie" to the Earls of Pembroke and Montgomery, Heminge and Condell explain that they have collected the plays "without ambition either of selfe-profit, or fame: onely to keepe the memory of so worthy a Friend & Fellow alive, as was our SHAKESPEARE, by humble offer of his playes, to your most noble patronage."

It is upon this not unexpectedly limited historical evidence that the controversy over the authorship of the Shakespearean plays and poems has nourished itself, feeding so well that the number of books and articles on the subject is almost beyond count. Paradoxically, the sceptics invariably offer as a substitute for the easily explained lack of evidence concerning William Shakespeare, the more troublesome picture of a vast conspiracy of silence about the "real author," with the total lack of historical evidence for the existence of this "real author" explained on the grounds of a secret pact, kept inviolate by a numerous and varied group of collaborators. In addition, they are all strong believers in the wonders of class distinctions, using the absence of sufficient information about William Shakespeare to paint a portrait of an illiterate, coarse buffoon incapable of even a flash of poetic feeling. Almost invariably this violent dislike of the man of Stratford is balanced by a frenzied worship of the sceptic's own candidate, who is drawn as a cultured, sensitive gentleman. But perhaps the most important characteristic shared by the "anti-Stratfordians," as they term themselves, is their unique concept of creative activity, a concept which not all of them are aware of embracing. Denying the role of vicarious experience in artistic creation, they believe, almost to a man, that a writer can describe only those things which he has directly experienced himself. This condition has been defined by one controversialist as "Literary Sincerity."

But the purpose of this brief survey is not to argue the merits of either side. Admittedly, though, the professors of English with their cabalistic reluctance to answer fully the charges of those writers who hold that Shakespeare did not compose the plays have made it difficult for the layman to understand the true nature of the unorthodox arguments. It is the modest hope of the author of this treatise that the brief history of the controversy which follows will provide such enlightenment. Far from exhaustive (it has been necessary, for example, to ignore almost completely the immeasurable amount of periodical literature on the subject), the survey is essentially representative in its emphases and its citations, and as accurate as the author's industry can make it.

Act I

THE DARK BACKWARD

Tempest, I, ii

The beginnings of the controversy are shrouded in time, and one speaks with small assurance in assigning to a single man the responsibility for first suggesting that William Shakespeare was an imposter. Although it has become fashionable for those opposed to the orthodox tradition to argue that the secret of the plays had been hinted at continuously from the late sixteenth century on, there is no overt evidence that Shakespeare's contemporaries saw anything unusual in the attribution of the plays to the Stratford actor and manager. One must, in fact, move on to the end of the seventeenth century, to a time when, ironically, many spurious plays were finding their way into the Shakespeare canon, to encounter the first clearly expressed doubts about the authorship. In 1687 a minor dramatist, Edward Ravenscroft, adapted *Titus Andronicus* for performance. In the address "To the Reader" of the printed edition, Ravenscroft, thinking it *"a greater theft to Rob the dead of their Praise then the Living of their Money"* confessed that there is *"a Play in Mr.* Shakespears *Volume under the name of* Titus Andronicus, *from whence I drew part of this."* Ravenscroft went on to reveal that *"I have been told by some anciently conversant with the Stage, that it was not Originally his, but brought by a private Author to be Acted, and he only gave some Master-touches to one or two of the Principal Parts or Characters; this I am apt to believe, because 'tis the most incorrect and indigested piece in all his Works; It seems rather a heap of Rubbish then a Structure."*

Ravenscroft, it should be noted, banished *Titus* from the canon as the result of a Bardolatry which refused to admit that Shakespeare could ever have written badly. His motives make him the first of the so-called Disintegrators, those orthodox Shakespeareans who, exploiting the uncertainties of Elizabethan theatrical history, would like to reduce the number of canonical plays to the few measuring up to the high standards of the greatest tragedies, histories, and comedies. Ravenscroft's example was followed by Alexander Pope, Samuel Johnson, and other eighteenth-century editors, who found it hard to accept the shoddier pieces of writing as Shakespeare's own. They, in turn, influenced the "modern" scholars of the nineteenth and twentieth centuries; and one of the ironical contrasts of our own day has been that of these orthodox writers fiercely guarding William Shakespeare from contamination by the lesser plays, while the Baconians and others protect these same plays from being soiled by association with the man of Stratford. None of the Disintegrators has ever doubted that Shakespeare was the author of the superior works, of course.

A rather different kind of comment upon the composition of the plays appeared in 1728 under the title of *An Essay Against Too much Reading.* Variously attributed to Matthew Concanen, a minor hack once satirized by Pope, and a certain Captain Goulding of Bath, the *Essay* presents the thesis that reading is the primrose path to failure as a writer. After pointing out how the study of Shakespeare "has frighten'd three parts of the World from attempting to write," the author discusses the more direct approach to literary composition utilized by the dramatist himself. Describing Shakespeare as a man who "was no Scholar, no Grammarian, no Historian, and in all probability cou'd not write *English*," he continues:

> I will give you a short Account of Mr. *Shakespear*'s Proceeding; and that I had from one of his intimate Acquaintance. His being imperfect in some Things, was owing to his not being a Scholar, which obliged him to have one of those chuckle-pated Historians for his particular Associate, that could scarce speak a Word but upon that Subject; and he maintain'd him, or he might have starv'd upon his History. And when he wanted any thing in his Way, as his Plays were all Historical, he sent to him, and took down the Heads of what was for his Purpose in Characters, which were thirty times as quick as running to the Books to read for it: Then with his natural flowing Wit, he work'd it into all Shapes and Forms, as his beautiful Thoughts directed. The other put it into Grammar; and instead of Reading, he stuck close to Writing and Study without Book. How do you think, Reading could have assisted him in such great Thoughts? It would only have lost Time. When he found his Thoughts grow on him so fast, he could have writ for ever, had he liv'd so long.

In his novel fashion, the author of *An Essay Against Too much Reading* also qualifies as an early Disintegrator.

In 1759 another minor dramatist, one James Townley, brought up the question of Shakespearean authorship again. The medium was a farce (sometimes attributed to the actor Garrick) entitled *High Life Below Stairs*. In this piece in which a group of servants ape the manners and activities of their masters, the following dialogue occurs between the *poseurs:*

Lady Bab's Maid: I'm afraid I have trespassed in Point of Time—
Looks on her Watch.—But I got into my fav'rite Author.
Duke's Servant: Yes, I found her Ladyship at her Studies this
Morning—Some wicked Poem—
Lady Bab's Maid: Oh you Wretch!—I never read but one Book.
Kitty: What is your Ladyship so fond of?
Lady Bab's Maid: *Shikspur.* Did you never read *Shikspur?*
Kitty: *Shikspur? Shikspur?*—Who wrote it?

Although the cautious have pointed out that this repartee
may simply represent the birth of an old and honorable
joke, other authorities have maintained that Townley's
farce marks the genesis of the movement to separate the
man of Stratford from the plays.

If James Townley was the first to ask—seriously or in
jest—who wrote Shakespeare, Dr. Herbert Lawrence was
the first to combine doubts about the authorship of the
plays with a personal attack upon the traditional author.
In 1769 Lawrence, a surgeon and apothecary given to the
pleasures of theatrical society, published anonymously *The
Life and Adventures of Common Sense: An Historical
Allegory,* a small volume of surprising popularity. The
modest title (Lawrence attempts to cover world history
from Ancient Greece to his own day) masks a puzzling
and frequently confusing first-person narrative in which
Common Sense tells the difficulties he has encountered in
making his way in the world. In one episode, he reveals
how his father, Wit, his father's crony, Genius, and his own
half-brother, Humour, arrive in London. Among their pos-
sessions are a commonplace book belonging to Wit; a glass
belonging to Genius; and a "Mask of curious Workman-
ship" belonging to Humour. All three of these objects possessed unusual powers. The commonplace book contained
"an infinite variety of Modes and Forms, to express all the
different Sentiments of the human Mind, together with
Rules for their Combinations and Connections upon every

THE

LIFE

AND

ADVENTURES

OF

COMMON SENSE:

An HISTORICAL ALLEGORY.

Veluti in Speculum.

Printed for MONTAGU LAWRENCE, Stationer,
At the Globe, near *Durham-Yard,* in the *Strand.*

MDCCLXIX.

Title page, *The Life and Adventures of Common Sense.*

12

Subject or Occasion that might Occur in Dramatic Writing," while the glass had "very extraordinary Properties," being the invention of Genius, who with its help could "even penetrate into the deep Recesses of the Soul of Man —could discover all the Passions and note their various Operations in the human Heart." Nor was the mask less astonishing, for "it has the Power of making every Sentence that came out of the Mouth of the Wearer, appear extremely pleasant and entertaining." Unfortunately these materials were soon stolen by "a Person belonging to the Playhouse; this Man was a Profligate in his Youth, and, as some say, had been a Deer-stealer, others deny it; but be that as it will, he certainly was a Thief from the Time he was first capable of distinguishing any Thing." Having frightened Wit, Genius, and Humour into leaving England, the thief proceeds to "examine the Fruits of his Ingenuity." The theft, Common Sense tells us, was known only to his Mother Truth, Wisdom, and himself, who agree "tho' much against my Mother's Inclination, to take no Notice of the Robbery, for we . . . were likewise apprehensive that we could not distress this Man without depriving his Country of its greatest Ornament." Common Sense then explains their reluctance more fully. "With these Materials, and with good Parts of his own, he commenced Play-Writer, how he succeeded is needless to say, when I tell the Reader that his name was *Shakespear.*"

Lawrence, whose book was long ignored, is now held by those among the learned who cannot take Townley seriously to have been the first to see through the Shakespearean imposture. The advocates of Francis Bacon go even further, labeling Lawrence the first Baconian. While admitting that their candidate is nowhere mentioned by name in *The Life and Adventures of Common Sense,* they point out that Bacon actually kept a commonplace book (now in the possession of the British Museum), and that this represents too striking a fact to be mere coincidence. Furthermore, they argue, Wit, Genius, and Humour (whom they confuse as one personage) represent known characteristics of Francis Bacon, clear indication that Lawrence was referring to their man. For the suggestion, made by some traditionalists, that Dr. Lawrence might merely have been committing a drollery, the Baconians have nothing but scorn. It is, therefore, of some interest that no one, apparently, has ever read more than a few pages of Dr. Lawrence's allegory, nor bothered to learn that Wit, Genius, and Humour are, along with the lady, Vanity, the villains of the tale, being held responsible for most of history's troubles. This would appear to be a point with which the Baconians ought to deal more fully.

Serious or not, Herbert Lawrence's attack on William Shakespeare reveals the personal hatred that will be so conspicuous a part of later attempts to dethrone the dramatist. Its allegorical nature is similar to that of another contemporary assault on the traditionalist position, made in a small volume which one scholar, in a masterpiece of understatement, labeled "another curious book of the late eighteenth century." *The Story of the Learned Pig, By an Officer of the Royal Navy* (1786) is a Pythagorean tale of the transmogrifications of a soul which, originally possessor of the body of Romulus, is at the time of the narrative dwelling in the performing pig on exhibit at Sadler's Wells. Usually resident in some meaner creature, the soul has had two other human moments in addition to its sojourn in the corpus of Romulus, having directed the destinies of Brutus and an Elizabethan ne'er-do-well known as Pimping Billy.

"I am now come to a period in which, to my great joy, I once more got possession of a human body. My parents, indeed, were of low extraction; my mother sold fish about the streets of this metropolis, and my father was a water-carrier; even that same water-carrier celebrated by Ben Jonson in his comedy of 'Every

Man in his Humour.' I was early in life initiated in the profession of horse-holder to those who came to visit the playhouse, where I was well-known by the name of 'Pimping Billy.' My sprightly genius soon distinguished me here from the common herd of that calling, insomuch that I added considerably to my income by standing 'pander,' as it is politely called, to country ladies and gentlemen who were unacquainted with the ways of the town. But this employment getting me frequently engaged in lewd quarrels, I was content to give it up at the expence of many a well-tanned hide. I soon after contracted a friendship with that great man and first of geniuses, the 'Immortal Shakspeare,' and am happy in now having it in my power to refute the prevailing opinion of his having run his country for deer-stealing, which is as false as it is disgracing. The fact is, Sir, that he had contracted an intimacy with the wife of a country Justice near Stratford, from his having extolled her beauty in a common ballad; and was unfortunately, by his worship himself, detected in a very aukward situation with her. Shakspeare, to avoid the conse-quences of this discovery, though it most prudent to decamp. This I had from his own mouth.

"With equal falshood has he been father'd with many spurious dramatic pieces. 'Hamlet, Othello, As you like it, the Tempest, and Midsummer's Night dream,' for five; of all which I confess myself to be the author. And that I should turn poet is not to be wondered at, since nothing is more natural than to contract the *ways* and *manners* of those with whom we live in habits of strict intimacy."

It seems almost superfluous to note that after this experience the quondam Billy found himself "turned into a bear."

To Common Sense and the Learned Pig is sometimes added the name of Horace Walpole as a third eighteenth-century iconoclast, although there appears to be no evi-dence in his writings to connect him with the movement to separate Shakespeare from the plays. The first two, es-pecially, are cited by dissenters as furnishing undeniable proof that the century had begun to see through the Shake-

speare imposture, and the allegorical nature of the pronouncements is defended on the grounds that the uncritical
(but by no means universal) admiration for "the man
Shakespeare" made open scepticism daring if not fool-
hardy. This being the case, much praise is due the next
figures on the scene, two men who were the first to argue
without allegorical coloring that William Shakespeare was
not the real author of the plays. Their theory, though not
made public until the beginning of the nineteenth century,
had its genesis late in the eighteenth.

The mind behind the theory was that of the Reverend
James Wilmot, D.D., who became rector of Barton on the
Heath, a small village just north of Stratford, in 1781.
Wilmot (whose niece styled herself Princess of Cumber-
land and claimed that her uncle had secretly married the
sister of Stanislaus, King of Poland, and was actually her
grandfather) was a strong admirer of the Shakespearean
literature and quite naturally found himself fascinated by
Stratford and its environs. Gradually, as his familiarity with
Shakespeare's country grew, he became convinced that the
Stratford citizen could not have written the plays. Wilmot's
reasons were two. The first was that he had searched every
private library within fifty miles of Stratford and had been
unable to find a single book which could be proved to have
been Shakespeare's; the second, that having discovered
Stratford to abound in colorful local legends, he had failed
to find any of this picturesque material in the plays. The
latter point he considered particularly impelling. According to Wilmot, there was one sixteenth-century legend of a
tall and ugly man who blackmailed the farmers under
threats of bewitching their cattle; another of the devil
removing a church tower; and a third of showers of cakes
falling at Shrovetide and crippling those whom they
chanced to hit. Emphasizing the highly dramatic nature of

these quaint myths, Wilmot argued that had Shakespeare actually written the plays he could scarcely have refrained from employing such vivid tales.

In a similarly direct manner Wilmot presented the claims of his own candidate, Francis Bacon, centering his argument that the great Elizabethan philosopher had written the plays on the belief that an allusion to the circulation of the blood in *Coriolanus* would be more likely to have come from the scientist Bacon than the thespian Shakespeare; and on the coincidence that the names of three characters in *Love's Labour's Lost* are those of three ministers at the court of Navarre, a court at which Bacon's brother had resided for a time. Thus Wilmot, rather than Lawrence, seems deserving of the title of the earliest Baconian, for as far as can be determined he was the first person to reject Shakespeare and accept Bacon on what purported to be reasonable grounds. Further credit is due him for establishing the essential pattern of the Baconian argument, a pattern consisting of expressed dissatisfaction with the number of historical records of Shakespeare's career, followed by the substitution of a wealth of imaginative conjectures in their place.

James Wilmot was a modest (or perhaps cautious) man and for twenty years he kept his beliefs to himself. Finally, insisting that his own name remain secret, he permitted a Mr. James Corton Cowell to disclose his views before a meeting of the Ipswich Philosophic Society on February 7, 1805. Cowell, readily confessing that he was "a Pervert, nay a Renegade to the Faith I have proclaimed and avowed before you all," and protesting that he was "prepared to hear from you as I unfold my strange and surprising story cries of disapproval and even of execration," told how the darkness surrounding Shakespeare's life had been suddenly dispelled by a "New Light." But, he continued, let me further confess that the author of this New Light was not myself but an ingenious gentleman of the neighbourhood of Stratford on Avon . . . I have not his permission to make public his name since as he rightly pointed out the Townsfolk of Stratford on Avon have of late years taken such a vast pride in the connexion of the Poet with their Town that they would bitterly resent any attempt to belittle the Poet.

Only after this careful prolegomenon did he reveal Wilmot's startling, although as we have seen, not wholly unanticipated, theory. It should be borne in mind that this moment marked, as far as can be ascertained, the first time that a man had dared to stand up in his own person and express his doubts (or anyone else's doubts) about the authorship of the Shakespeare canon. Apparently, Wilmot's heresy did, as Cowell had feared, provoke cries of disapproval, for in April Cowell attempted to strengthen his radical position by revealing the name of the true author of the theory, having first sworn each and every member of the meeting to secrecy. The secret was successfully kept until 1932 when the keen eye of a Shakespearean scholar lit upon the unpublished manuscripts of Cowell's two speeches. The faithful silence of the members of the Ipswich Philosophic Society offers an interesting commentary on the awful nature of the revelations afforded them by the rector of Barton on the Heath.

Thus by the beginning of the nineteenth century Shakespeare's claims to the plays and poems had been explicitly, if only semipublicly, challenged, and the name of Sir Francis Bacon seriously advanced as substitute author. For the next forty years there was a kind of buzzing in the air, although no one appeared in print with anything resembling the Wilmot-Cowell thesis. But reading the literature of the period, one is aware of an increasing impatience with the traditional picture of the actor-manager Shakespeare, an impatience surely a direct result of the uncritical adulation

Portrait of Mrs. Constance Pott, from Ignatius Donnelly, *The Great Cryptogram* (R. S. Peale and Co., 1888).

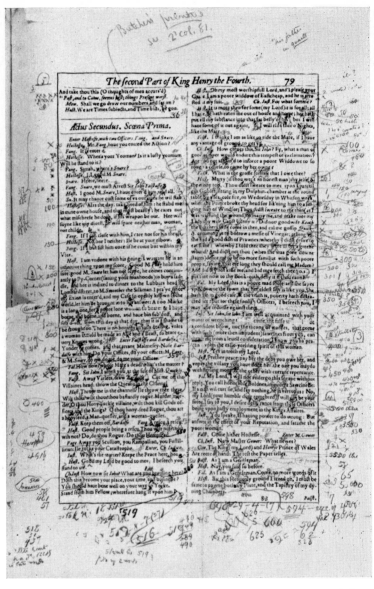

Facsimile of page of 1623 Folio used by Ignatius Donnelly as a worksheet, from *The Great Cryptogram* (R. S. Peale and Co., 1888).

Photograph of Dr. Orville W. Owen's WHEEL, from *Sir Francis Bacon's Cipher Story* (Howard Publishing Co., 1894).

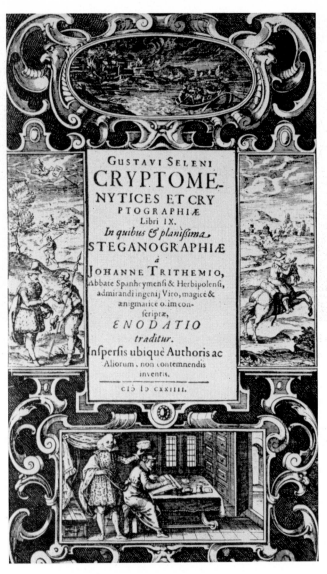

Title page, "Gustavi Seleni Cryptomenytices et Cryptographiae," from Sir Edwin Durning-Lawrence, *Bacon Is Shake-speare* (John McBride Co., 1910).

The Lichfield Chapter House Cleavage, from Walter Conrad Arensberg, *The Burial of Francis Bacon and His Mother in the Lichfield Chapter House.*

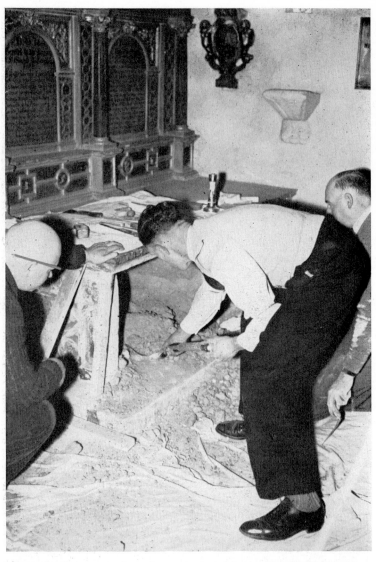

Calvin Hoffman's search in the sand of Sir Thomas Walsingham's tomb.
United Press Photograph.

Calvin Hoffman peering into the empty tomb of Sir Thomas
Walsingham. United Press Photograph.

that the Shakespearean works had been afforded by romantic writers in England, America, and especially Germany. Shakespeare the writer had become the very embodiment of poesy to the Romantics; he could do no wrong and brooked no peer. Yet the historical man had, all too obviously, feet of clay. In 1811, Coleridge, as devout a Shakespearean as one could wish, expressed his amazement that "works of such character should have proceeded from a man whose life was like that attributed to Shakespeare," and in 1837 a character in Disraeli's *Venetia* asked, rather ungrammatically: " 'And who is Shakespeare? We know as much of him as Homer. Did he write half the plays attributed to him? Did he ever write a single whole play? I doubt it!' " Without insisting that Disraeli was a Baconian, we can admit the probability that the question of authorship was in the air when *Venetia* was composed. That America too had difficulty in reconciling the man and the poet is shown by Emerson's lecture, delivered in the winter of 1845–46. Concerning the biography of Shakespeare, he confesses:

The Egyptian verdict of the Shakspeare Societies comes to mind; that he was a jovial actor and manager. I can not marry this fact to his verse. Other admirable men have led lives in some sort of keeping with their thought; but this man, in wide contrast. Had he been less, had he reached only the common measure of great authors, of Bacon, Milton, Tasso, Cervantes, we might leave the fact in the twilight of human fate: but that this man of men, he who gave to the science of mind a new and larger subject than had ever existed, and planted the standard of humanity some furlongs forward into Chaos,—that he should not be wise for himself;—it must even go into the world's history that the best poet led an obscure and profane life, using his genius for the public amusement.

Here, clearly stated, is the romantic dilemma. The attempts to solve it will be the theme of the rest of this book.

The romantic dissatisfaction of the beginning of the nineteenth century came to a head in 1848 with the appearance of a document of major importance in the history of the Shakespearean controversy. The author was an American, Colonel Joseph C. Hart, an officer in the National Guard and a New York lawyer. Hart set forth his views in a volume rather curiously entitled *The Romance of Yachting,* a book marking the first time that the traditionalist position had openly (without benefit of allegory) been challenged in print.

There is no uncertainty in Hart's expression of his views. Apparently an incorrigible iconoclast and chauvinist (in the same volume he attacks the traditional view of New England's historical importance, concluding that "New England and her Puritans were more than *a full century behind New-York* and her people, in every thing that is of value in civil and religious liberty and progressive civilization"), Hart was also a man of impressive self-confidence, for he states in his preface that "this Volume of the Romance of Yachting will probably fall into the hands of most persons of intelligence going to sea . . . and it is likely, also, that it will form an addition to nautical libraries generally." While admitting that *The Romance of Yachting* contains some unusual observations, he bravely asserts that he "holds himself responsible, for all his opinions, at the bar of enlightened and manly criticism." He then proceeds to narrate an exciting Atlantic crossing on a yacht named the *J. Doolittle Smith* and his subsequent arrival in Spain. It is while reminiscing about this particular land of romance that the subject of Shakespeare comes up, for having noted that the Spanish river Guadalete is actually the mythological Lethe "corrupted by the common Moorish prefix," Hart is led by a consideration of the subject of forgetfulness to *The Winter's Tale* and to the nonexistent seacoast of Bohemia. This, in turn, brings him to the authorship of the plays.

After "the bard" had been dead for one hundred years and utterly forgotten, a player and a writer of the succeeding century, turning over the old lumber of a theatrical "property-room," find bushels of neglected plays, and the idea of a "speculation" occurs to them. They dig at hazard and promiscuously, and disentomb the literary remains of many a "Wit" of a former century, educated men, men of mind, graduates of universities, yet starving at the door of some theatre, while their plays are in the hands of an ignorant and scurvy manager, awaiting his awful fiat. They die in poverty, and some of absolute starvation. Still their plays, to the amount of hundreds, remain in the hands of the manager, and become in some way or other his "property." A "factotum" is kept to revise, to strike out, to refit, revamp, interpolate, disfigure, to do any thing to please the vulgar and vicious taste of the multitude. No play will succeed, without it is well peppered with vulgarity and obscenity. The "property-room" becomes lumbered to repletion with the efforts of genius. It was the fashion of the day for all literary men to write for the theatre. There was no other way to get their productions before the world. In the process of time, the brains of the "factotum," teeming with smut and overflowing all the while with prurient obscenity, the theatre becomes indicted for a nuisance, or it is sought to be "avoided" by the magistrates for its evil and immoral tendency. The managers are forced to retire; and one, who "owns all the properties," leaves the hundreds of original or interpolated plays to the usual fate of garret lumber, some with the supposed *mark* of his "genius" upon them. They are useless to him, for he is a player and a manager no longer. A hundred years pass, and they and their reputed "owner" are forgotten, and so are the poets who wrote and starved upon them. Then comes the resurrection—*"on speculation."* Betterton the player, and Rowe the writer, make a selection from a promiscuous heap of plays found in a garret, nameless as to authorship. "I want a hero!" said Byron, when he commenced a certain poem. "I want an author for this selection of plays!" said Rowe. "I have it!" said Betterton; "call them Shakspeare's!" And Rowe, the "commentator," commenced to puff them as "the bard's," and to write a history of his hero in which there was scarcely a word that had the foundation of truth to rest upon.

"This," concludes Hart quietly, "is about the sum and substance of the manner of setting up Shakspeare."

Hart then elaborates upon Shakespeare's role as "the mere 'factotum' of a theatre," employed to vulgarize the products of other men's genius. "The plays he purchased or obtained surreptitiously, which became his 'property,' and which are now called his, were never set upon the stage in their original state. They were first spiced with obscenity, blackguardism and impurities, before they were produced; and this business he voluntarily assumed, and faithfully did he perform his share of the management in that respect" for "it brought *money* to the house." As a result of William Shakespeare's peculiar form of employment, "we can easily discover the part he wrote by its filth" and can say without hesitation that, vulgarities and obscenities excepted, the plays could not possibly be his. Hart is willing to make just one exception, *The Merry Wives of Windsor,* for if "any play of the whole catalogue is Shakspeare's, this comes nearest the mark. The impress of his vulgar and impure mind is upon every page."

Hart did not, as is sometimes stated, reveal who the real authors were, nor does the name of Francis Bacon get anything but passing mention. Indeed, he admits quite freely that the "enquiry will be, *who were the able literary men who wrote the dramas imputed to him* [i.e., Shakespeare]?" and he implies that such inquiry had already begun when he comments that the old joke from *High Life Below Stairs* causes " 'not so much laughing as formerly.' " One suspects, however, that his own favorite was Ben Jonson, whom he describes as "the only man of that day, of poetical power sufficient to write the higher parts" of *Hamlet.* The lower part (consisting of the gravedigger scene) he gives to Shakespeare, labeling it "the Shakspearian blot."

There can be no doubt about Joseph Hart's place in literary history. Not only was he the first person to state explicitly and unequivocally in print that William Shakespeare did not write the plays bearing his name, but also he developed at length the important thesis that Shakespeare was, in Hart's own words, "a vulgar and unlettered man." With Hart, it is interesting to note, Emerson's romantic uneasiness about Shakespeare's "profane life" has become a form of social snobbery according to which only the university graduate can be an educated man (an attitude that ignores the great classical scholarship of the nonuniversity writer, Ben Jonson). Furthermore, the angry tone and the personal animus exhibited against Shakespeare were to become major characteristics of the arguments advanced by Hart's followers. Colonel Hart's religious fervor rather than the Reverend Mr. Wilmot's gentle scepticism was to be the mark of the iconoclast from this time forth.

The next eight years were relatively quiet, with the only excitement provided by Dr. R. W. Jameson's suggestion, made in 1852 in *Chamber's Edinburgh Journal,* that Shakespeare produced his plays by "keeping his poet." But in 1856 there appeared on the scene two writers whose published views on the question provoked immediate, angry, and frequent response, a reception noticeably different from the lack of interest shown toward Hart's earlier announcement. This response seems to justify the assertion that the controversy over the authorship of the Shakespearean plays actually began with the writers' appearance in print. Perhaps prophetically, the almost simultaneous publication of their somewhat similar theories culminated in a battle over priority, and ugly charges of plagiarism (later retracted) were made against the English writer by no less a person than Nathaniel Hawthorne. Prophetic too was the striking contrast in methodology between the two heretics, the Englishman relying upon historical and literary conjecture to make his case, his American counterpart depending on cryptographical revelations for hers. These two methods remain to this day the fundamental approaches to the problem of dethroning Shakespeare.

Since the lesser known of the two iconoclastic students of Shakespearean biography wrote in 1857 that "if it were necessary I could show, that for upwards of twenty years I have held the opinion that Bacon was the author of the Shakespeare plays," we will begin with him. William Henry Smith, a man who when not tilting at Shakespearean windmills was apparently something of a recluse, has been described as a person of "peculiar" education, having been "thrown very much upon himself and upon a few books . . . Burton's *Anatomy of Melancholy* and *The Pilgrim's Progress* for his theology; Bacon for his solid reading, Shakespeare for his lighter studies." It was this intellectual diet (and the necessity of finding a suitable topic for a youthful debating attempt) that led him to the conviction that Francis Bacon rather than William Shakespeare was the author of the plays. In 1856 Smith published his theory (for private circulation) in the form of a letter to Lord Ellesmere, then head of the Shakespearean Society. A year later he enlarged the pamphlet to a small book setting forth his ideas in some detail and following an argumentative method soon to be embraced by other sceptics. The book begins with a demonstration of our ignorance of Shakespeare's life, devoting an entire chapter to this crucial point. I quote the chapter in full.

A BRIEF HISTORY OF SHAKESPEARE.

WILLIAM SHAKESPEARE's is indeed a negative history.

Of his life, all that we positively know is the period of his death.

We do not know when he was born, nor when, nor where, he was educated.

We do not know when, or where, he was married, nor when he came to London.

We do not know when, where, or in what order, his plays
were written or performed; nor when he left London.
He died April 23rd, 1616.

In fact, writes Smith in a subsequent chapter of *Bacon And
Shakespeare,* all we know of William Shakespeare is that
he was one of those "licensed Vagabonds" who called themselves actors. Orthodox scholars, needless to say, consider
this history skeletal if not defeatist. Nevertheless, it is fundamental to Smith's argument, for he next proceeds to
demonstrate that we know quite a bit about Bacon's life,
which, interestingly enough, he finds paralleling Shakespeare's in many ways.

His next step is to show that Bacon's unique wit is revealed in the plays. Quoting Macaulay's statement that "if
by wit be meant the power of perceiving analogies between
things which appear to have nothing in common, he [Ba-
con] never had an equal; not even Cowley—not even the
author of *Hudibras,"* Smith points out that the plays reveal a mind that leaves no analogy unnoticed. Therefore,
according to the logic of Macaulay's statement, Bacon must
have written the plays. Smith sums up his case as follows,
calling to mind Wilmot and Cowell in his preference for
a wealth of conjecture to a more modest amount of fact.

Thus we see that Bacon and Shakespeare both flourished at the
same time, and might, either of them, have written these works,
as far as dates are concerned, and that Bacon not only had the
requisite learning and experience, but also that his wit and poetic
faculty were exactly of that peculiar character which we find exhibited in these plays.

Introducing the element of artistic personality, Smith but-
tresses his argument with a device soon to become a favorite, the citation from Bacon and Shakespeare of passages
revealing similarities of idea and expression. He notes, for
example, that Bacon's apophthegm, "For there be many

wise men that have secret hearts, but transparent coun-
tenances," is curiously echoed in *Henry IV, Part II:* "And
the whiteness of thy cheek, / Is apter than thy tongue to
tell thy errand." He is much impressed, too, by the fact
that both Shakespeare and Bacon use the word "inkling."
These and many other equally striking parallels are cited
by Smith as irresistible proof that the philosopher wrote the
plays.

Smith does admit that there is some evidence in Shakespeare's favor; the "fact of his name always having been
attached to and associated with" the plays, and Ben Jonson's repeated references to him. The first difficulty Smith
dismisses quite arbitrarily, but his handling of the second
is ingenious. Maintaining that Jonson's complimentary
poem in the First Folio is "capable of a double meaning,"
he gives the following demonstration.

Jonson:

> Soul of the age!
> Th' applause, delight! the wonder of our age,
> My Shakespeare—rise!

Smith:

> "Soul of the age" seems a term more applicable to Bacon
> than to Shakespeare; whilst the possessive pronoun "my,"
> added to Shakespeare, may serve to render his invocation
> applicable to either the one or the other.

Jonson:

> Thou art a monument without a tomb,
> And art alive still while thy book doth live,
> And we have wits to read, and praise to give,

Smith:

> The lines . . . seem much more applicable to a living
> than to a deceased person.

Jonson:

> And though thou hast small Latin and less Greek,
> From thence to honour thee I would not seek
> For names.

Smith:

> . . . We do not undertake to prove that Bacon had "small
> Latin and less Greek," but simply to suggest, that these
> lines might possibly refer to him [for, as Smith had writ-
> ten a few lines earlier] a man might have a very
> considerable knowledge of Latin and Greek, and yet
> be pronounced by so finished and critical a scholar as Ben
> Jonson undoubtedly was, to have "small Latin and less
> Greek."

Among those impressed by the power of Smith's arguments was the great Lord Palmerston, who is reported to
have ended a discussion over the authorship by thrusting
Bacon And Shakespeare at his opponents and remarking,
"read that, and you will come to my opinion."

It is not William Henry Smith, however, but the Ameri-
can lady who caused him so much embarrassment who is
popularly supposed to have been the originator of the
Baconian theory. Yet her great fame is more the result of her own tragic intensity than of her theories, for
Delia Bacon was, as we have seen, neither the first to doubt
Shakespeare, nor the first to suggest Francis Bacon in his
place. She was, in the strictest sense of the word, not even a
Baconian, having been what unorthodox writers term a
Groupist; that is, one who believed that the plays were written by more than a single person. According to Delia Bacon
they had actually been composed by a coterie of playwrights, led by Sir Walter Raleigh, and inspired by the poetic and philosophical genius of Sir Francis Bacon. But in
spite of this divided allegiance, Delia Bacon is generally

regarded as having been her namesake's greatest champion.

Born in Ohio, daughter of one clergyman and sister to another (and not descended from Sir Francis), Delia Bacon found success in New England as a lecturer and teacher of history. Her happiness was short-lived, however, having been shattered first, it is said, by a heartless "young theologian" who, for the amusement of his friends, allowed her to think that he was interested in marriage; and then by the derision to which her Shakespeare theories exposed her. Her ideas were first made public in an essay published in *Putnam's Monthly Magazine* in 1856 (some eight months before the appearance of Smith's "Letter"). The editor timidly emphasized that he was "disclaiming all responsibility" for its "startling view of the question." Delia Bacon asked (in a somewhat emotional manner) how much longer "shall we be able to accept in explanation of it [i.e., the authorship] . . . the story of the Stratford poacher?" She blasted at tradition by describing mankind as "condemned to refer the origin of these works to the vulgar, illiterate man who kept the theatre where they were first exhibited. . . . Condemned to look for the author of Hamlet himself—the subtle Hamlet of the university, the courtly Hamlet, 'the glass of fashion and the mould of form'—in that dirty, doggish group of players, who come into the scene summoned like a pack of hounds to his service." And she concluded that had we "but applied to these works the commonest rules of historical investigation and criticism," the results would have been the discovery, "ere this," of

ONE, with learning broad enough, and deep enough, and subtle enough, and comprehensive enough, one with nobility of aim and philosophic and poetic genius enough, to be able to claim his own, his own immortal progeny—undwarfed, unblinded, undeprived of one ray or dimple of that all-pervading reason that informs them; one who is able to re-claim them, even now, "cured and perfect in their limbs, and absolute in their numbers, as he conceived them."

This is the conclusion of her first article. Unfortunately the editor of *Putnam's Monthly* lost his nerve and declined to print its successor, with the result that she had to wait until her book, *The Philosophy of the Plays of Shakspere Unfolded,* appeared in 1857 to divulge the name of the ONE. By this time, however, the ONE had become the many, although a single figure, Francis Bacon, was held to be the intelligence most directly responsible for the plays.

Delia Bacon's thesis is complex and at times difficult to follow, a difficulty suggested by such subheadings as Book II, Part I, "Lear's Philosopher; (Or, The Law Of The 'Special And Respective Duties,' Defined And 'Illustrated' In Tables Of 'Presence' And 'Absence.')." According to her theory, Bacon and a group of kindred spirits described as "Raleigh's School" conceived a new philosophy which they proceeded to transmit to posterity, not only explicitly in Bacon's known philosophical writings but implicitly in the Shakespearean plays. The theory is set forth in her introduction, a part of which is given below. The reader will, it is hoped, bear with the rather lengthy quotations; such primary evidence seems to be the only way of conveying the essence of Delia Bacon's argument with any accuracy.

The proposition to be demonstrated in the ensuing pages is this: That the new philosophy which strikes out from the Court— from *the Court* of that despotism that names and gives form to the Modern learning,—which comes to us from the Court of the last of the Tudors and the first of the Stuarts,—that new philosophy which we have received, and accepted, and adopted as a practical philosophy, not merely in that grave department of learning in which it comes to us professionally *as* philosophy, but in that not less important department of learning in which it comes to us in the disguise of amusement,—in the form of fable and allegory and parable,—the proposition is, that this Elizabethan philosophy is, in these two forms of it,—not two philosophies,—not two Elizabethan philosophies, not two new and wondrous philosophies of nature and practice, not two new Inductive philosophies, but one,—one and the same: that it is philosophy in both these forms, with its veil of allegory and parable, and without it; that it is philosophy applied to much more important subjects in the disguise of the parable, than it is in the open statement; that it is philosophy in both these cases, and not philosophy in one of them, and a brutish, low-lived, illiterate, unconscious spontaneity in the other.

The proposition is that it proceeds, in both cases, from a reflective deliberative, eminently deliberative, eminently conscious, *designing* mind; and that the coincidence which is manifest not in the design only, and in the structure, but in the detail to the minutest points of execution, is *not* accidental.

Just why these eminent men decided upon so indirect a method of revealing themselves to posterity Delia Bacon explains in some detail. According to her,

It was a time when authors, who treated of a scientific politics and of a scientific ethics internally connected with it, naturally preferred this more philosophic, symbolic method of indicating their connection with their writings, which would limit the indication to those who could pierce within the veil of a philosophic symbolism. It was the time when the cipher, in which one could write *'omnia per omnia,'* was in such request, and when 'wheel ciphers' and 'doubles' were thought not unworthy of philosophic notice. It was a time, too, when the phonographic art was cultivated, and put to other uses than at present, and when a *'nom de plume'* was required for other purposes than to serve as the refuge of an author's modesty, or vanity, or caprice. It was a time when puns, and charades, and enigmas, and anagrams, and monograms, and ciphers, and puzzles, were not good for sport and child's play merely; when they had need to be close; when they had need to be solvable, at least, only to those who *should* solve them. It was a time when all the latent capacities of the English language were put in requisition, and it was flashing and crackling, through all its lengths and breadths, with puns and quips, and conceits, and jokes, and satires, and inlined with philosophic secrets that opened down 'into the bottom of a tomb'—that opened into the Tower—that opened on the scaffold and the block.

Miss Bacon then reminds the reader that this new philosophy was not easily unearthed.

The great secret of the Elizabethan age did not lie where any superficial research could ever have discovered it. It was not left within the range of any accidental disclosure. It did not lie on the surface of any Elizabethan document. The most diligent explorers of these documents, in two centuries and a quarter, had not found it. No faintest suspicion of it had ever crossed the mind of the most recent [*sic*], and clear-sighted, and able investigator of the Baconian remains. It was buried in the lowest depths of the lowest deeps of the deep Elizabethan Art; that Art which no plummet, till now, has ever sounded. It was locked with its utmost reach of traditionary cunning. It was buried in the inmost recesses of the esoteric Elizabethan learning. It was tied with a knot that had passed the scrutiny and baffled the sword of an old, suspicious, dying, military government—a knot that none could cut—a knot that must be untied.

The great secret of the Elizabethan Age was inextricably reserved by the founders of a new learning, the prophetic and more nobly gifted minds of a new and nobler race of men, for a research that should test the mind of the discoverer, and frame and subordinate it to that so sleepless and indomitable purpose of the prophetic aspiration. It was 'the device' by which they undertook to live again in the ages in which their achievements and triumphs were forecast, and to come forth and rule again, not in one mind, not in the few, not in the many, but in all. 'For there is no throne like that throne in the thoughts of men,' which the ambition of these men climbed and compassed.

The principal works of the Elizabethan Philosophy, those in which the new method of learning was practically applied to the noblest subjects, were presented to the world in the form of AN

ENIGMA. It was a form well fitted to divert inquiry, and baffle even the research of the scholar for a time; but one calculated to provoke the philosophic curiosity, and one which would inevitably command a research that could end only with the true solution. That solution was reserved for one who would recognise, at last, in the disguise of the great impersonal teacher, the disguise of a new learning. It waited for the reader who would observe, at last, those thick-strewn scientific clues, those thick-crowding enigmas, those perpetual beckonings from the 'theatre' into the judicial palace of the mind. It was reserved for the student who would recognise, at last, the mind that was seeking so perseveringly to whisper its tale of outrage, and 'the secrets it was forbid.' It waited for one who would answer, at last, that philosophic challenge, and say, 'Go on, I'll follow thee!' It was reserved for one who would count years as days, for the love of the truth it hid; who would never turn back on the long road of initiation, though all 'THE IDOLS' must be left behind in its stages; who would never stop until it stopped in that new cave of Apollo, where the handwriting on the wall spells anew the old Delphic motto, and publishes the word that *'unties* the spell.'

Such a one Delia Bacon conceived herself to be.

Both her style and her arguments make Miss Bacon's reasoning difficult to follow, but the ensuing extract will give some idea of how she pursued her theories. Maintaining that Bacon in both his acknowledged and unacknowledged writings revealed himself as strongly interested in the "Cure of the Common-Weal," she argues that:

No man suffered death, or mutilation, or torture, or outrage of any kind, under the two tyrannies of this age of learning, that it was possible for this scientific propounder of the law of human *kind*-ness to avert and protect him from—this anticipator and propounder of a *human* civilization. He was far in advance of our times in his criticism of the barbarisms which the rudest ages of social experiment have transmitted to us. He could not tread upon a beetle, without feeling through all that exquisite organization which was great nature's gift to her Interpreter in chief, great nature's pang. To anticipate the sovereign's wishes, seeking to divert them first 'with a merry conceit' perhaps; for, so light as that were, the motives on which *such* consequences might depend then—to forestall the inevitable decision was to arm himself with the powers he needed. The men who were protected and relieved by that secret combination against tyranny, which required, as the first condition of its existence, that its chiefs should occupy places of trust and authority, ought to come out of their graves to testify against the calumnies that blast our modern learning, and the virtue—the virtue of it, at its source. Does any one think that a universal *slavery* could be fastened on the inhabitants of this island, when wit and manliness are at their height here, without so much as the project of an 'underground rail-way' being suggested for the relief of its victims? 'I will seek him and *privily* relieve him. Go *you* and *maintain talk with the Duke* that my charity be not of him *perceived*. If he ask for *me*, I am ill and gone to bed. Go to; say you nothing. There is division between the Dukes—[between the Dukes]—and a worse matter than that. I have received a letter this night. It is *dangerous to be spoken*. I have *locked the letter* in my *closet*. There is *part* of *a power already* FOOTED. We must incline to THE KING. If I die for it, as no less is threatened me, the king, *my old master,* must be relieved.' *That* when all is done will be found to contain some hints as to the manner in which 'charities' of this kind have need to be managed, under a government armed with powers so indefinable.

Some of the difficulty encountered in trying to follow Delia Bacon's thesis may come from her book's being admittedly incomplete, lacking that "HISTORICAL KEY" which was originally the principal part of her study. This omission caused her to conclude by noting that "the objection to the work here presented to the public is, that it does not go far enough." She explains that omission, however, by noting that, while the "Historical Part of this work" had been "for a long time completed and ready for the press,"

It seemed better to save to the world the power and beauty of this demonstration, its intellectual stimulus, its demand on the judgement. It seemed better, that the world should acquire it also in the form of criticism, instead of being stupified and over-powered with the mere force of an irresistible, external, historical proof. Persons incapable of appreciating any other kind of proof, —those who are capable of nothing that does not 'directly fall under and strike *the senses,*' as Lord Bacon expresses it,—will have their time also; but it was proposed to present the subject first to minds of another order.

Although Nathaniel Hawthorne, who wrote a preface to it (but did not, as is frequently asserted, agree with Delia Bacon's thesis), once remarked that "I believe that it has been the fate of this remarkable book never to have had more than a single reader," the volume is actually one of the landmarks among iconoclastic studies, having popularized speculation about the authorship in a way that none of the early pronouncements, including Smith's, had. Even more important than the excitement caused by *The Philosophy of The Plays of Shakspere Unfolded* was the example of single-minded devotion to the cause revealed by its writer. While her volume was still in press, she journeyed to Stratford, seeking positive proof of her theory. For months she haunted the grave of Will the Jester (as she frequently called Shakespeare), convinced from her reading of "Lord Bacon's" letters that under the gravestone would be found the archives of the Elizabethan group responsible for the plays. Finally, it is claimed, she received the Vicar's permission to open the grave, only, at this critical moment, to be assailed by serious doubts. Had she clearly understood the cryptic message of the letters? Was it Shakespeare's grave that was meant? Or Raleigh's? Or Spenser's? Or Bacon's? According to the evidence of her friends, the tragic climax to Delia Bacon's career came one night when, lantern in hand, she entered the church at Stratford and for long hours stared at the tomb in dreadful indecision. Hawthorne reported that she actually felt of the stones, satisfying herself that her strength was sufficient to raise them. But at the crucial moment her courage failed her and she retired from the church a broken woman. By the time her book had appeared, she was violently insane and had to be carried home to America by a nephew returning from China. She died in the "Retreat" at Hartford in 1859. It was suggested by some of her critics that her rapid deterioration had been caused not only by her doubts about the tomb, but also by a suspicion coincident with the publication of her book that her theory was all wrong. True or not, it is a fact that since Delia Bacon's time few of Shakespeare's detractors have doubted the accuracy of their own deductions.

In spite of the ridicule and abuse with which *Bacon And Shakespeare* and especially *The Philosophy of The Plays of Shakspere Unfolded* were greeted by traditionalists, the search for the "real" author of the Shakespearean plays now became a popular international pastime. Although an occasional Elizabethan was to get passing notice, the only serious contender from 1857 to the end of the century was Francis Bacon, whose supporters soon divided themselves into two camps, the one favoring the relatively straightforward argumentative methods of William Henry Smith, the other drawn to the more complex and mysterious ways of Delia Bacon. But both groups would retain in common certain significant characteristics inherited from their progenitors: the strong dislike for the figure of the Stratford man, so marked in Hart and Delia Bacon; the compensating love, ecstatic in its fervor, for one's own candidate, most noticeable in Delia Bacon's case; the caste-consciousness, able to associate nobility of spirit only with gentle blood and university education, inferable from the arguments of Wilmot through Delia Bacon. Most important, they would agree, as did the sceptics already dealt with, that to try to relate the wonders of the Shakespearean plays to the banal realities of recorded history was to defy the very idea of poetic genius.

Act II

TO WORSHIP SHADOWS

Two Gentlemen of Verona, IV, ii

Sir Francis Bacon's popularity as a candidate for Shake-speare's laurels can be explained in part by his eminent position in Elizabethan history. However, it certainly owes something to the felicitous appearance of Spedding's monumental edition of his writings, the first volume of which arrived at the bookstalls in the very year (1857) that William Henry Smith and Delia Bacon were calling attention to the great philosopher. At precisely the right moment there began to be generally available a vast storehouse of information about Bacon's activities. Of particular importance were his letters, notably one addressed to John Davies published by Spedding in 1868, in which Bacon had requested Davies "to be good to concealed poets." On the basis of this rather obscure phrase, his adherents were quick to assume that Bacon was referring to himself, a not inexplicable assumption, for it enabled them to meet one of the most serious objections to Bacon's candidacy, the fact that nothing in his extant writings indicates that he was possessed of poetical powers.

But Bacon's advocates did not wait for the completion of Spedding's edition to continue the battle. First to seize the somewhat tattered banner from Delia Bacon was William D. O'Connor, described by a thorough historian of Baconianism as author of the "first book ever published, subsequent to the utterances of Delia Bacon and William Henry Smith, in which the Baconian theory was advocated." The book, published in 1860, was actually a novel, *Harrington: A Story of True Love.* Not only does its hero utter Baconian sentiments, but O'Connor himself admits his admiration for and indebtedness to Delia Bacon in a note at the end of the book, stating it as his personal opinion that the reader will "find it more to his profit to be insane with her, on the subject of Shakespeare, than sane with Dr. Johnson." The writer of this challenging statement was a man of varied talents. In addition to several later contributions to the Baconian cause, including the provocatively entitled *Hamlet's Notebook* (1886), O'Connor was sometime Corresponding Clerk of the Lighthouse Board in Washington and author of the poem, "To Fanny." A friend of Walt Whitman, he wrote *The Good Gray Poet,* a volume whose title made an indelible impression on the American public. And not his least claim to fame is Hawthorne's eulogy of him as the only person who had ever "positively" read Delia Bacon's book from "end to end."

While William D. O'Connor had been trifling with fiction, a more serious mind had been mulling over the rival claims of Shakespeare and Bacon. In 1866 there appeared the fullest and most judicial presentation of the Baconian thesis to date, its author (often styled the "apostle of Baconianism") the Honorable Nathaniel Holmes, its title *The Authorship Of Shakespeare.* Judge Holmes (no relation to Oliver W.), who became Professor of Law at Harvard soon after the appearance of his book, argued that Francis Bacon was the true and sole author of the Shakespearean plays, insisting that "in short, Bacon's prose is Shakespearean poetry, and Shakespeare's poetry is Baconian prose."

Judge Holmes' arguments have a familiar ring. Not only was his legal mind incapable of accepting the proposition "that the spontaneous genius of a born poet, without the help of much learning, should come to see deeper into all the mysteries of God, Nature, and Man, and write better about the universal world, than the most accomplished scholars, critics, and philosophers," but he found it equally difficult to accept Hart's theory that Shakespeare had been a kind of editor or vulgarizer of the plays, "that a common under-actor should turn poet, and, rummaging over the hereditary lumber of the play-house, should gather up the best of the traditional material, and through the limbec of his capacious brain distil the quintessence of British genius from time immemorial." Thus, it followed logically to Judge Holmes that if Shakespeare could not have written the plays, Bacon, the most learned philosopher of his day (and a lawyer to boot) must have. The thorny problem of why Bacon should have wished to conceal his authorship Holmes solved simply, maintaining that in the beginning Bacon was "a briefless young barrister, who did not desire to be known as a writer for the stage" because he knew that this kind of notoriety would be fatal for a budding lawyer and politician. Later, when Bacon's wisdom had seen the folly of worldly fame, he cared "but little for any lustre that might be added to his name, or his memory, by these writings," and so the "arrangement" made early in his life to have the *"factotum"* Shakespeare take on the plays and poems as his own was never altered.

Judge Holmes, as had William Henry Smith, leaned heavily upon parallel expressions to strengthen his thesis. He pointed out that "swelling" was a "favorite word" with both Shakespeare and Bacon; that the noun "toys" and the verb "toss" were "much used by both"; that "level" was a "favorite expression" of both. For him, these similarities of diction were certain proof that one man must have written Bacon's works and Shakespeare's plays. That man could not have been Shakespeare.

The judicial, reasonable tone of Holmes' book is in the spirit of William Henry Smith, rather than of the mystical Delia Bacon. It is explained by a later Baconian, who stated that "one has but to look at the portrait of Judge Holmes, which we present herewith, to read the character of the man—plain, straightforward, honest and capable." It should be noted, however, that the judge's appearance was not considered unusual in a man opposed to the Stratford tradition, for the writer continues:

In fact, I might here observe that it seems to me that all the portraits of the original Baconians presented in this volume are remarkable for the intellectual power manifested in them. A finer collection of faces never adorned the advocacy of any theory. Instead of being, as the light-headed have charged, a set of visionaries, their portraits show them to be people of penetrating, original, practical minds, who differ from their fellows simply in their power to think more deeply, and in their greater courage to express their convictions.

Delia Bacon's portrait does not appear in this particular volume.

Up to this time the Bacon-Shakespeare controversy had apparently been confined to Great Britain and America. In 1878 the first French Baconian made his appearance when M. J. Villemain published two articles in *L'Instruction Publique*. M. Villemain's conclusion is worth quoting: "En résumé, on pourrait conclure ainsi: Tout ce qu'il y a de bon dans les drames de Shakespeare, est de Bacon; tout ce qu'il y a de mauvais dans les drames de Bacon, est de Shakespeare." In the same year Dr. William Thomson, an

Antipodean medical man interested in the causes of phthisis, brought Australia into the picture with *The Political Purpose of the Renascence Drama*. Dr. Thomson, described by a contemporary as a man whose "usefulness as a member of society was somewhat marred by his quarrelsome disposition," believed the plays to contain hidden historical allusions which, properly understood, revealed Bacon as the author. Thomson subsequently published numerous books and pamphlets in defense of his ideas; among them might be mentioned *Bacon and Shakespeare on Vivisection* and *A Minute Among the Amenities*. But his energy never gained him the stature enjoyed by the next dissenter of note, the American, Appleton Morgan. Morgan, A.M., LL.B., and author of several legal treatises, attempted in *The Shakespearean Myth* (1881) to destroy the Shakespeare legend rather than to advance the claims of anyone else. Although he believed that the plays were written by a group which included Southampton, Raleigh, Essex, Rutland, Montgomery, and Bacon (whom he described as "needy and ambitious"), he denied that he was a Baconian and devoted the better part of his energy to showing that Shakespeare was merely a theatrical handyman who had gained a "proprietary" interest in the plays by readying them for the stage. His theories were not, as we have seen, particularly novel, yet the book is an interesting one, raising a number of legitimate historical questions, most of which modern scholarship claims to have answered. It is interesting that as the years passed, Morgan, although remaining convinced that more than one man had a hand in the plays and that Bacon had some connection with the issuance of the First Folio, became increasingly orthodox, arguing against the Baconians with as much vigor as he had once demonstrated against the traditionalists. Certainly his interest in the Shakespearean works went far beyond the mere question of authorship, as is evinced by the Shakespeare Society of New York which he was instrumental in founding in 1885. Under the aegis of the Society, Morgan published what must surely be the most elaborate edition of Shakespeare ever undertaken by amateurs, *The Bankside Shakespeare,* whose twenty-some expensively printed volumes were edited by, in addition to Morgan himself, an impressive array of doctors, lawyers, and clergymen.

In the meantime the ladies were beginning to interest themselves in speculation as to the author. Best known was the Englishwoman, Mrs. Henry Pott. Inclined early in her career to the methodology of her countryman, William Henry Smith, rather than that of her feminine predecessor, Delia Bacon, Mrs. Pott brought forth in 1883 an edition of Bacon's *Promus of Formularies and Elegancies,* a commonplace book largely in Bacon's handwriting (now part of the Harleian collection of the British Museum). Consisting of notes and quotations, the manuscript was "illustrated and elucidated by passages from Shakespeare" by the editor, who was struck by the phenomenon that many of the proverbs, biblical verses, and well known quotations found in the *Promus* also appear in the plays. She concluded, as a result, that Bacon not only wrote the plays, but through them was responsible for enriching the English language with what a fellow Baconian described as "those beautiful courtesies of speech"—"'Good morrow,' 'Good day,' etc."

Mrs. Pott soon followed her edition of the *Promus* with a pamphlet, entitled *Did Francis Bacon Write "Shakespeare"? Thirty-Two Reasons For Believing That He Did.* The lady's first three reasons are typical:

(1) That no facts have yet been discovered concerning the lives of either Bacon or Shakespeare which render it impossible that Bacon should have written the Plays.

(2) That many particulars in the circumstances under which the Plays are known to have been produced or acted, as well as the chronological order and dates attributed to the several Plays

and Poems by Dr. Delius . . . coincide with the facts in the life of Bacon.

(3) That the hints which the Plays and Sonnets contain of their author's experiences, mental and physical, are infinite in number when applied to the life and experiences of Francis Bacon, but can with difficulty be strained so as to show any connection with or self-illustration of Shakspere.

Mrs. Pott gives "EXAMPLES" for many of her *"Reasons."* One will suffice here.

(28) That the superstitions, as well as the religious beliefs and opinions on Church matters, as well as the study of the Bible, which is so clearly traceable in the Plays, are plainly acknowledged by Bacon.

EXAMPLE:—Only one small but curious instance can be offered on this vast subject. Bacon told the king that he feared that the wedding-ring was becoming an object of too much respect, almost of superstition. There is not one mention in the Plays of a wedding-ring. *Bacon didn't wear one*

While Dr. Thomson and Mrs. Pott were concerning themselves with routine investigations of hidden historical allusions and with verbal and conceptual parallels, an American lady, Mrs. C. F. Ashmead Windle, had been engaged in more exciting research. Mrs. Windle, who lived in San Francisco but reminded her readers that she was "Of Philadelphia," had been struck by Delia Bacon's reference to a cipher veiling the great "ENIGMA." Moved by "the magic music" in her "heart," she took it upon herself to penetrate the "VEILED ALLEGORY" of the plays. Her penetration revealed Bacon to be the true author. According to Mrs. Windle, the texts of the plays contained carefully worked out secret messages which could be understood only when the reader became aware of the true meaning of certain key words. (Future refinements of Mrs. Windle's relatively simple cipher would include the substitution of other characters for the letters intended, transposing the letters after arranging them in blocks, using a substitute alphabet, etc. Needless to say, the skill necessary to have given any cipher the textual appearance of a Shakespearean play would have been considerable.) In 1881 she published her "under-reading" of *Cymbeline* in the form of an open *Address* to the *"Gentlemen of the New Shakspere Society of London."* A year later, having apparently been ignored by the *"Gentlemen,"* she published a *Report* to the *"Trustees of the British Museum, on behalf of the Annals of Great Britain, and the Reign of Her Majesty, Queen Victoria,"* in which she announced the *"Discovery And Opening"* of Bacon's cipher in six more plays and in Montaigne's *Essays.* In her own words,

I shall now proceed to open the same Cipher in these dramas, absolutely disclosing Lord Verulam as their author, and tossing the artificial Shakespeare to the winds of his ridicule. It is a Cipher, which in them, as I need not say to you, has heretofore eluded the research of two hundred and fifty years, under the study of diligent investigators, and which has totally escaped the notice of the most diverse and voluminous commentators. Nevertheless, as patiently and passively as the sleeping princess of the legend awaited the arrival of the true knight destined to awake her with his kiss, so has it lain ready to respond to the mutual touch. And, even as by "the magic music in his heart" it was, that true knight snapped the spell, aroused the lady fair, and with her the slumbering retinue of the enchanted palace, that

> "All the long-pent stream of life
> Dashed downward in a cataract,"

so do I, by the same power, stir the cabala of this long stilled volume, flutter its gentle "Ariel" to start the warders, plume his own pinions, and warble his native notes, that echo take up the strain, and reverberate the miracle of Verulam through "the flutes and trumpets" of perpetual time.

Mrs. Windle's method of opening the cipher is so un-usual that it warrants a rather lengthy citation. I give here the first part of her "under-reading" of *Othello,* the play she considered to be the basis of the cipher. It is presented ver-batim and literatim, only the peculiarities of nineteenth-century type having been occasionally modernized.

OTHELLO

A tale, oh! I tell, oh!
Oh, dell, oh! What wail, oh!
Oh, hill, oh! What willow! *
What hell oh! What will, oh!
At will, oh! At well, oh!
I dwell, oh!

[I do not assume to give definitely, or to exhaust nearly all the catches that may be snatched from the title of this, or any other of the weird and wondrous titles of these dramas. They are meant to be snggestive [*sic*] of the spirit presence of the author, and they must necessarily be adapted to more or fewer changes, according to the measure of the mind and ear to which they address them-selves. To attempt to limit them, either in sound or sense, would be to materialize them, and entirely to lose the ideal and super-sensuous effect which belongs to them. Each reader, when once initiated, will ring his own changes, for such was the great author's design. Their scope is confined as earth, or expansive as air—as cabined as mere words, or as exalted as the thought to which the words are but the base-round of an interminable ladder reaching to Heaven, whereon each is invited to step and ascend as far as his individual capacity may enable him to conjoin language with that infinitude which he can still never begin to express.   C. F. A. W.]

---

* That this particular catch was designed by the author is proven in Desde-mona's song of the "Willow."

Table of Invention† as Key to Othello.

THE DUKE OF VENICE: Judgment.†

MONTANA [*sic*]: The watchword of a Discovery.

Clues to the Watchword.

MICHAEL: Referring to Michael de Montaigne.

A FLORENTINE: Referring to Florio's translation of Montaigne's Essays.

ARITHMETICIAN: } Referring to the chapter on *Names* in
See me aright on title.}   Montaigne's Essays.

BRABANTIO: } The question of Bacon's authorship of the
Brabble on't you, O!}   plays, arising from tokens in Othello.

CYPRUS: }
Cypress.* } Information of a *Cipher* in the dramas, with ap-
Cipher us. }   peal to unfold it, so as to elicit sympathy on
Sigh for us. }   the disclosure.

VENICE: }
Come here. } The word *Venice* may recall the author's early
Come see. }   poem, "The *Venus* and Adonis."
Venus. }

---

† Notes.—"For we form a history, and *tables of invention* for anger, fear, shame and the like, and the mental operations of memory, composition, *judgment,* and the like, as well as for heat and cold, light and vegetation, and the like."—*Novum Organum.*

> "Thy gift, thy tables, are within my brain,
> Full *charactered* with lasting memory."—*Sonnet* 122.

> "This Tablet lay upon his breast,
> Wherein our pleasure his full fortune doth confine."—*Cymbeline.*

* Notes.—"And keep Invention in a noted weed. (Cypress is the symbol of grief, as we say "widow's weeds," and the pun, of which the author's Cipher is formed, was a rank "weed" in Bacon's day.) That every word doth almost tell my name, showing their birth (derivation), and where they did proceed (analogy and reference)."—*Sonnet* 76.

"I have (though in a despised weed) procured the good of all men."
Prayer found among Bacon's Papers.

IAGO: ⎤   Bacon wills to let "go" his poetical reputation, that
I ago.† ⎢   through thus following the eternal Divine
Ay, ay, go. ⎢   Will,† it shall go down to posterity.
Ay, I go. ⎦

DESDEMONA: ⎤
With a demon A.‡ ⎬ The double tragedy of Bacon's Muse.
With a moan, ah! ⎦

BIANCA: ⎤
Buy on care. ⎬ Bifold modes of Bacon's Muse.
Buy on cure. ⎦

CASSIO: ⎤   *Cause* of Bacon's *casing* himself, or concealing
Case you, oh! ⎬   his authorship of the plays, which will
Cause you, oh! ⎦   prove by the clue to be found in this play,
                     to have been the *cause* of his country—a
                     sacrifice after the manner of some instances
                     cited by Michael de Montaigne.

LODOVICO: ⎤   Bacon the *Viceroy* of a lode of ore, sup-
Vice o' lode, oh! ⎬   pressed by a vicarious *load* of sorrow.
Vicarious load, oh! ⎦

GRATIANO: ⎤   *Great*ness and *grace* accumulating to Bacon
Great you on, oh! ⎬   from the course he wills to pursue.
Grace you on, oh! ⎦

EMILIA: ⎤ The expression of Bacon's *ill,* continued in play
I'm ill, you. ⎬   after play, as *mile*-stones of his life.
I mile you. ⎦

---

† See Sonnets 134, 135, 136, 142.

† See Old Testament, Book of Daniel, Chap. VII, ANCIENT OF DAYS.

‡ NOTE.—This refers to the Moor Aaron, in *Titus Andronicus,* and is shortly explained.

ERRATUM. *Omitted from the above Table of Invention:*

OTHELLO: ⎤
Hot hell, oh! ⎬ The anguish of Bacon's sacrifice, as told in the tragic dramas.
Oh, tell, oh! ⎦

RODERIGO: } *Road* toward death to present fame in the
Road where I go. }   plays, for the sake of the future; in short, Bacon's road toward the destiny of his choice.

RELATED CLUES.

WILL: Referring to the autograph of William Shakespeare in the transmitted copy of Florio's Montaigne.

THE MOOR: Referring to the *Titus Andronicus.*

MARCUS LUCICOS: Referring to the *Titus Andronicus.*

ANGELO: Referring to *Measure for Measure* and *Comedy of Errors.*

TURKS: Referring to Ciphers in the *Merchant of Venice.*

OTTOMITES: Referring to Ciphers in the *Merchant of Venice.*

ALEPPO: } Referring to the *Merchant of Venice.*
A lip, O. }

In putting the names of the *dramatis personae* into the Cipher (its mode being already learned from the *De Augmentis*), where there is still any uncertainty left as to the absolute symbol, we can assure ourselves by noticing the language of what is spoken in the dialogue by the character of which we are doubtful.

At the opening of this play we are immediately introduced to Cassio, with the prefix of another name—one not given him on the list of *dramatis personae,* and therefore not in Cipher, but to be noted as important; for at once Iago propounds two conundrums concerning him, the first as spoken by Othello:

"*Othello.*   For certes, says he,

    I have already chose my officer."

And the next as by himself:

"*Iago.*   Forsooth, a great *arithmetician,*

> One *Michael* Cassio, a *Flor*entine.
> A fellow almost damned in a fair wife." *

This, in connection with the translation of Cassio by the Cipher into *Case you, oh! Cause you, oh!*

> "*Oth.*   It is the *cause*, it is the *cause*, my soul—
>   Let me not name it to you, you chaste stars.
>   It is the *cause*,"

is set down in our minds for consideration, as we connect it with the prefix *Michael*, while we at the same time recognize a familiarity in *Michael* and *Flor*, as coming thus in juxtaposition, and feel that the full reminiscence will presently come to us, realizing it to be of peculiar importance in the Cipher.

Iago lets us know that he also is important here, for he begins to give us riddles about himself:

> "*Iago.*   Were I the Moor I would not be Iago,
>   In following him, I follow but myself."

And again:

> "*Iago.*   I am not what I am."

There is, too, an enigma in his title of officer to Othello—"his ancient." This is a familiar word; we remember it as used in the Bible, look it up in Daniel, the seventh chapter, and learn it means the Supreme Authority. Pursuing Iago in the dialogue we soon find him discoursing on the *will*, and get this word as the application of his cipher, in its variations, not forgetting among these that Will is the old generic name for a poet, and also that it is connected especially with *William Shakespeare*, through certain punning sonnets ascribed to him in his day, as well as through a similar punning passage in the play of *Much Ado About Nothing*.

Brabantio is another to utter riddles. He says:

> "*Brab.*   These sentences, to sugar, or to gall,
>   Being strong on both sides, *are equivocal*."

---

* Note.—This line is in reprehension of that which detracts from the value of Montaigne's Essays—the book is spoken of under the figure of a wife.

Thus we learn that, as *a brabbler,* he stands for *the opened question of the true authorship of the dramas.*

Desdemona, as well, proclaims herself a sphinx, under own protest:

"*Des.*   I do beguile
          The thing I am by seeming otherwise."

Othello says, mysteriously:

"*Oth.*   *I must be found,*
          My parts, my title, and *my perfect soul,*
          Shall manifest me rightly."

And again:

"*Oth.*   *Your mystery, your mystery;* nay, dispatch."

And yet again:

"*Oth.*   Were it *my cue.*"

We have, moreover, Cassio with his hand to his mouth, in token of secrecy, as spoken by Iago:

"*Iago.*   It had been better you had not *kissed your three fingers so oft.* * * * Very good, well kissed! an excellent courtesy: 'tis so, indeed: yet again, *your fingers to your lips.*"

And Iago saying, in token of silence:

"*Iago.*   *Lay thy finger thus.*"

And swearing something *double:*

"*Iago.*   By *Janus!*"

And asking:

"*Iago.*   How comes this *trick?*"

Emilia says, too:

"*Emil. Turn the key.*"

So that there is the stirring of mystery and secrecy continually suggested in this drama. We also find the following intimation that this is the play in which to open the Cipher:

"We must not think the Turk is so unskillful
To leave that latest *which concerns him first.*"

The following:

"*Iago.*   Here's a goodly *watch* indeed!
Who's that *which rings the bell?*"

And this:

"*Mon.*   Come, let's set the *watch,*"

explain MONTANO as a *watchword,*

Then presently we have *the coupling* of the words *Michael* and *Montano,* with a hint for the memory:

"*Oth.*   How comes it, *Michael,* you are *thus forgot?*

"*Cas.*   I pray you pardon me, I cannot speak.

"*Oth.*   Worthy *Montano,* you were wont be civil:

*   *   *   *   *   *

What's the matter
That you unlace your reputation thus,
And *spend your rich opinion for the* NAME
Of a night brawler?"

With this the familiar "Michael," which we could nevertheless not place at the beginning, comes to us as the prenomen of a writer somehow mixed up in our minds with these dramas, namely: as that of MICHAEL DE MONTAIGNE, so fitting for us the lingual root of *Mon*-tano. As we are told that Michael Cassio was a *Flor*-entine, we hereupon immediately think of *Florio's* translation. Then rushes upon us the recollection that there is preserved in the British Museum a copy of this edition containing, in autograph, the name of *William Shakspere.*

Having thus connected the Verulamiam Cipher with that relic, we have caught the cue intended in Cipher of this drama.

The authenticity of the British Museum signature has been challenged by prominent paleographers.

By this time the controversy was becoming a matter of international concern, and Wyman's bibliography of it, published in 1884, lists two hundred and fifty-five titles attacking and defending Shakespeare. Among these were notices from Germany, France, Italy, Holland, and India, as well as from various parts of the British Empire and from the United States. Germany had already produced its first Baconian, the anonymous author of "Shakspere's Geheimnisz und Bacons 'Promus'" which appeared in *Allgemeine Zeitung* for March 1, 1883. But it was in America that the Bacon-Shakespeare battle had most captured the public's fancy, a fact borne out by the preponderance of American titles (almost two-thirds the total number) in Wyman's bibliography. American interest in the question is further shown by such evidence as the *New York Herald*'s series on the controversy which appeared in September and October, 1874, and by the amusing article in the *Harvard University Bulletin* of April 1, 1881, entitled "Is there any doubt as to the Authorship?" and described by Wyman as "a short list of the references for the use of students in debate."

Furthermore, a recognizable pattern to the supporters of the negative side was beginning to emerge. The proposition that Shakespeare was an imposter had a strong appeal to the professional mind, it is clear, with lawyers and medical men leading the way, followed rather distantly by members of the clergy. It is worth remarking in this respect that the first two professions, at least, require rigorous training, a background that might well make one unsympathetic to the concept of natural genius. The proposition appealed to a different kind of mind, also, to the idealistic, mystical intelligence of the female student of literature, whose obvious weaknesses as an amateur historian were more than compensated for by untrammeled imagination. Apparent, too, as one surveys these mid-Victorian dissenters is their middle-class background. Indeed, it appears to be a not unsafe generalization to observe that the entire controversy has been a kind of middle-class affair. I am not aware that either the peer or the peasant has been particularly bothered by the problem of Shakespeare's humble beginnings.

But to return to our narrative. William Henry Burr, an American gentleman who not only believed that Bacon was Shakespeare, but that Tom Paine was "Junius" and had written the Declaration of Independence, brought out the first of his several books on the authorship in 1883. Four years later his countryman, H. L. Hosmer, published a study of the sonnets which "were undoubtedly written for the purpose of conveying to future ages the true history of the dramas." Complaining that the poems had been given merely "a literal interpretation," Hosmer devised a key to unlock their secret. Its use revealed "all the real facts concerning the composition of the works attributed to Shakespeare, the reason for transferring the authorship to him, and the manner in which it was done." The key, as it appears in *Bacon And Shakespeare In The Sonnets,* is given below in its entirety.

KEY.

Thou and Thine......	Impersonation of Truth.	
Thy and Thee	"	" Thought in the abstract.
Thyself	"	" Thought in delineation.
You and Your	"	" Beauty in the abstract.
Yourself	"	" Beauty in delineation.
I, My, Mine, Me......	"	" Bacon in person.
Myself	"	" Bacon as author.
My Love	"	" The dramas.
My Friend	"	" Shakespeare.
My Mistress	"	" Tragedy.

It will be noted from the next to last item that Hosmer's Bacon had a certain affection for William Shakespeare, more than that displayed by most of his advocates. The reason, Hosmer informs us, was that Shakespeare, although chosen by Bacon "because of his capacity for money getting," was not really a bad sort, having been "true, honest, faithful, and thrifty." Hosmer even goes so far as to defend him from charges of a dissolute youth, maintaining that he "was no worse than nine tenths of the young men who permit themselves to be swayed by passion and a love of notoriety."

In the meantime Bacon's English followers were not inactive. In 1885 The Bacon Society was founded, promising to publish "from time to time" a journal for the discussion of major issues. Entitled *Baconiana* in 1892, the journal has appeared regularly ever since. By 1888 interest had reached such a pitch that a "selection" of letters on the subject to the *Daily Telegraph* filled a good-sized volume entitled *Dethroning Shakspere,* edited by R. M. Theobald, Honourable Secretary to The Bacon Society. Mrs. Ashmead Windle's name was not included among the letter writers, although her cipher theories were the subject of much discussion. They appeared, modified but not acknowledged, as the discoveries of the American, Ignatius Donnelly, a name soon to become one of the most important in the long history of the authorship question. Basing his analysis of the plays on what is perhaps the most ingenious and elaborate cipher ever presumed to have been constructed by the mind of man, Donnelly claimed (as had Mrs. Windle) to have found irrefutable evidence of Bacon's authorship in cryptic utterances running through the dramas. These discoveries, revealed to Appleton Morgan as early as 1885, were first set forth in an exploratory article in the *North American Review* in 1887 (the year that Hugh Black discovered a cipher in Shakespeare's epitaph) and then propounded fully in 1888 in an enormous volume of nine hundred and ninety-eight pages called *The Great Cryptogram.*

Donnelly, known as the "Great Apostle of Protest" for

his contributions to the People's Party (or "Populists" as the members were generally known), was one of the most amazing men ever to decorate the American scene. A lawyer who found study of the law dull, he became one of the great visionaries of his time. Among his many accomplishments was the creation of a Utopia, the astounding Nininger City in Minnesota. Here Donnelly's dream of a community where cultural activity and the hard physical labor of the frontier could go hand in hand became a brief reality, until the crash of 1857 and its ensuing panic brought the dream to an end. Donnelly also served terms as lieutenant governor and member of Congress for Minnesota. In 1882, having been temporarily eased out of politics, he retired to his house amid the ruins of Nininger City and began his literary career in earnest. His first effort was *Atlantis: The Antediluvian World,* demonstrating the truth of Plato's tale of a sunken continent and showing that this sea-washed civilization and the Garden of Eden were one and the same. The next year, in *Ragnarok, The Age of Fire and Gravel,* he demonstrated that the composition of the earth had been affected by collision with a mighty comet. Five years later he brought forth *The Great Cryptogram.*

Donnelly's volume consists of three books, "The Argument" in which he sets forth the traditional objections to Shakespeare and the claims of Bacon, "The Demonstration" in which he unfolds the cipher "narrative," and "Conclusions," a brief summing-up. In the first he places great emphasis on parallelisms as proof of the common authorship of the Baconian and Shakespearean writings, finding, for instance, that "the word *infinite* is a favorite with both writers," as is the metaphor, to "purge." Similarly, he is impressed by the strikingly identical opinions of Shakespeare and Bacon; for example, the belief that nature is superior to art. But, weighty as Donnelly's list of parallelisms may be, it is in "The Demonstration" that the true heart of his theory is to be found.

"The Demonstration" is Donnelly's reading of Bacon's cipher as it is woven into the concluding pages of *Henry IV, Part I* and the opening pages of *Henry IV, Part II,* using the 1623 Folio as a text. The "cipher narrative" tells a strange tale of Bacon's authorship and of court gossip and intrigue. Donnelly's chapter heads are interesting and informative in this regard: "Cecil Tells The Story Of Marlowe;" "The Story Of Shakspere's Youth;" "The Queen Beats Hayward;" "Cecil Says Shakspere Did Not Write The Plays;" "Shakspere Incapable Of Writing The Plays;" and so forth. The narrative is not at all flattering to Shakespeare, who is described by Lord "Seasill" as a "poor, dull, ill-spirited, greedy creature, and but a veil for some one else, who had blown up the flame of rebellion almost in to war against your Grace as a royal tyrant." (It might be mentioned that the lines just quoted represent a conversation between Bacon's enemy, Lord Cecil, and Queen Elizabeth.) Among other bits of historical information the narrative details the murder of Christopher Marlowe, revealing a version of the affair which modern scholarship claims to have shown to be at variance with the actual facts of the case.

Donnelly does not give the whole key to the cipher, confessing that "all I give is reality; but I may not give all there is." What he does give is so complex as to be difficult to describe, for while his method is based on counting words, he does not hesitate to reverse his technique and count up the page instead of down, or backwards instead of forwards, when his narrative thread appears to have disappeared. But his own description of how he stumbled upon the cipher will make the true nature of his method more apparent than any editorial comment.

Being satisfied that there was a cipher in the Plays, and that it probably had some connection with the paging of the Folio, I turned to page 53 of the Histories, where the line occurs:

I have a gammon of BACON and two razes of ginger.

I commenced and counted from the top of the column downward, word by word, counting only the spoken words, until I reached the word Bacon, and I found it was the 371st word.

I then divided that number, 371, by fifty-three, the number of the page, and the quotient was seven! That is, the number of the page multiplied by seven produces the number of the word *Bacon*. Thus:

$$\begin{array}{r} 53 \\ \times\ 7 \\ \hline 371 \end{array}$$

This I regarded as extraordinary. There are 938 words on the page, and there was, therefore, only one chance out of 938 that any particular word on the page would match the number of the page.

Donnelly also considered it a "curious fact, that while the tenth word from the top of a column was, of course, the tenth word, you could not obtain the tenth word from the bottom of a column by deducting ten from the total of words on that column." These and other mysterious features of the 1623 Folio convinced Donnelly of the existence of a hidden message.

Donnelly's reading of the cipher has been criticized for his failure to make the key wholly known to his readers. The importance of this failure can be appreciated when one realizes that he attempted to enlarge the Baconian canon to include not only the known works of Shakespeare, but practically all the dramatic pieces of the Elizabethan era. Donnelly was quite certain that Bacon wrote *The Arraignment of Paris, Arden of Feversham, George-a-Greene, Locrine, King Edward III, Mucedorus, Sir John Oldcastle, Thomas Lord Cromwell, The Merry Devil of Edmonton, The London Prodigal, The Puritan, A Yorkshire Tragedy, Fair Em, The Birth of Merlin,* the lost *Love's Labors Won* and *Duke Humphrey,* to name but a few. Nor was he at all unsympathetic to Mrs. Pott's suggestion (made to him in a private letter) that the hand of Bacon could be seen in the plays of Marston, Massinger, Middleton, Greene, Shirley, and Webster; and he pointed out that had Bacon "dashed off" a play every two weeks between 1581 and 1611 he could have written *"seven hundred and eighty plays!"* Certainly Bacon could not have afforded to dawdle over his work, for he was also, according to Donnelly, the true author of Christopher Marlowe's plays, Burton's *The Anatomy of Melancholy,* and Montaigne's *Essays,* not to mention various minor productions of the Elizabethan era. His arguments for the Baconian authorship of Montaigne's essays are particularly challenging. Pointing out that both Bacon and Montaigne believed that had man more "senses" he could apprehend "things in nature now hidden from us," Donnelly concludes:

In short, we are brought face to face with this dilemma: either Francis Bacon wrote the *Essays* of Montaigne, or Francis Bacon stole a great many of his noblest thoughts, and the whole scheme of his philosophy, from Montaigne. But Bacon was a complete man; he expanded into a hundred fields of mental labor. Montaigne did nothing of any consequence to the world but publish these *Essays; ergo:* the great thoughts came not from Montaigne to Bacon, but from Bacon to Montaigne.

The importance of Donnelly's theories can be measured by the number of imitations they inspired. Sparked by his electric, if incomplete, ideas, an army of scholars began to search for a more satisfactory cipher, with the result that occultism became a major characteristic of Baconian activity from 1888 on. Among the countless decipherers were some whose energy and imagination caused them immediately to be recognized as leaders of this particular branch of research. One such was W. F. C. Wigston. Author as early as 1884 of a preliminary investigation of the Bacon secret, Wigston published in the year of *The Great Cryptogram* a study entitled *Bacon, Shakespeare, and the Rosicrucians.*

Owing much to Delia Bacon, his theory held that the plays had been written by the learned members of a secret society named for a fifteenth-century German nobleman, Christian Rosenkreuz. Initiates included Sidney and Jonson, with Shakespeare acting as a front for the group. The real leader and true inspirer of the society was Bacon, however. When the more or less simultaneous appearance of Donnelly's immense volume made his own arguments for the arcane qualities of the plays seem superficial, if not unnecessary, Wigston turned his attention to proving Bacon's influence on the Rosicrucians and to deciphering the cryptic messages in Bacon's *known* writings. In *Francis Bacon Poet, Prophet, Philosopher Versus Phantom Captain Shakespeare The Rosicrucian Mask* published in 1891 (and dedicated to Donnelly), Wigston learnedly discussed Bacon's relationship to the Rosicrucians and to Freemasonry, building his case on long and untranslated citations of obscure German and Latin authorities. Some idea of his energy can be gained from the knowledge that between 1888 and 1892 he published six books on this difficult and recondite subject.

Similar in many respects was the labor of a Rochester, New York, lawyer, John Elisha Roe, who in *The Mortal Moon; or, Bacon and His Masks: The Defoe Period Unmasked* (1891) carried on the task of enlarging the number of Bacon's works. Although it might seem to the uninitiated that Ignatius Donnelly had left little for his successors to accomplish in this respect, Roe proposed some startling additions to the accepted canon, including works hitherto thought to have been by Philip Stubbs, Robert Burton, Jonathan Swift, Addison and Steele, and, of course, Daniel Defoe. In *Sir Francis Bacon's Own Story* (1918) Roe added Milton, Thomas Cromwell, Thomas Hobbes, and Carlyle to his list. All these were, it should be understood, in addition to Shakespeare. Furthermore, Roe contended, Bacon did not die in 1626 but lived on secretly, serving as "covert secretary and mouthpiece to Cromwell, and to that secret knot of sturdy Englishmen including Rawley, John Milton and others; who, had it been possible, would have placed him as Francis 1st of England."

By a curious coincidence, the year of *The Mortal Moon* saw the reappearance of Mrs. Pott who had abandoned the prosaic methods of the William Henry Smith "school" for the more exciting type of research started by Delia Bacon. The not wholly original thesis of *Francis Bacon and His Secret Society* was that Bacon had founded the Rosicrucian Society, the Shakespearean plays being merely one part of his recondite scholarship for that brotherhood. The existence of a secret message in the plays became therefore not only logical, but even necessary. In the second edition of her work she made some interesting additions to her theory, stating, for example, that Bacon began to "draw together his *'Invisible Brotherhood,'* the Rosicrucian Fraternity" at the "age of 15," a bit of information that "was positively asserted and enforced with instances by a Rosicrucian, *the last of his circle,* to the present writer." Anticipating Roe was her assertion that Bacon did not really die in 1626, that

In 1626 he died to the world—retired, and by the help of many friends, under many Names and Disguises, passed to many Places. As Recluse, he lived a life of study; revising a mass of works published under his "Pen-names"—enlarging and adding to their number. They form the Standard Literature of the 17th Century.

She also claimed for Bacon "the great works of the 16th" century. Mrs. Pott was not absolutely sure just when Bacon did die, but she appears to have inclined toward 1668, a date on which he would have been one hundred and seven.

Not all Bacon's advocates were prepared to base their case on the existence of a cipher, however. Edwin Reed, for example, one of whose many studies, *Bacon vs. Shakspere:*

Brief for Plaintiff, apparently first appeared prior to 1890 and was, expanded and revised, to know at least seven more editions by 1898, was not an active member of the cipher school. A moderately worded study (but one which actually added nothing new to the Baconian argument), Reed's book drew its strength from its simple insistence that (1) Francis Bacon was a poet and (2) the literary styles of the plays and of Bacon's acknowledged works were the same. To support the former contention Reed quoted Bacon's beautiful lines, "The world's a bubble, and the life of man / Less than a span." To lend force to the latter, he cited various parallel passages, such as "Pride must have a fall" (Shakespeare) and "Pride will have a fall" (Bacon). Reed was also impressed by Shakespeare's large vocabulary, said by some authorities to total twenty-one thousand words.

Who was it, living in England in the latter part of the sixteenth and the early part of the seventeenth centuries, that compassed so enormous a range of diction? Was it William Shakspere, the actor, born and bred in what Halliwell-Phillips called a "bookless neighborhood" . . . ?

Let us rather turn to the man who at the age of twelve entered Cambridge University; who at fifteen exhausted that fount of learning, and left it without taking his degree. . . .

The idea of a "bookless neighborhood" is developed by Reed at some length in connection with *Venus and Adonis,* a "product of the highest culture."

Is it possible that in a town where six only of nineteen aldermen and burgesses could write their names, where the habits of the people were so inconceivably filthy that John Shakspere, father of William, was publicly prosecuted on two occasions for defiling the street in front of his house, where the common speech was a *patois* rude to the verge of barbarism, and where, probably, outside of the school and church, not a half-dozen books . . . were to be found among the whole population,—is it possible that in this town a lad of twenty composed this beautiful epic?

Or is it possible, as some defenders of John's son have maintained, that the fact of John's prosecution suggests that Stratford was as well policed as Hollywood, or Paris, or any other city famed for its inspiration to artists?

Among other writers avoiding the extreme claims of the Wigston-Roe-Pott school was Thomas W. White, who in *Our English Homer* relieved Shakespeare of the plays, but distributed them with admirable fairness among the better-known Elizabethan dramatists, reserving for Francis Bacon only *Hamlet* and five lesser plays as of his "entire composition." Writing in 1892 and obviously impressed by the discoveries of contemporary classical scholarship, White maintained that some of the plays were based directly or indirectly upon Roman and Greek originals, and that all were at best rewritings either of Italian, Spanish, and classical dramas, or of the works of contemporary and classical historians. Among the "revisers" he cited Greene, Marlowe, Chapman, Peele, Daniel, Nashe and Lodge, in addition to Bacon. *Hamlet* he held to be an adaptation of Sophocles' *Electra,* and not a very good one at that.

Now, everybody must see that the adapter has made very felicitous use of the materials afforded by the Greek tragedy; but no one at all familiar with dramatic literature can fail to perceive at the same time that he was a novice in the art of dramatic composition; while every classical scholar will be struck by the fact that, though we have much beautiful diction of his own, he nowhere reproduces the splendid declamation of his model.

Of Hamlet's first soliloquy White noted, for example, that "the opening is simply ridiculous, suggesting that there is no alternative to suicide, but running to water like rotten ice." However, White could not bear to have even this bit of bathos associated with the name of Shakespeare, whom he characterized as "of a grossly animal disposition." But this keen sally at the expense of the Stratford actor did not save White's book from scathing reviews from the pens of more orthodox iconoclasts, who, understandably, did not take kindly to attacks on the plays themselves.

Also worthy of mention as a conservative heretic is Reed's fellow American, Theron S. E. Dixon, who demonstrated in *Francis Bacon and His Shakespeare* that *The Tempest* is pure Bacon. The following gloss upon a key passage (Dixon apologizes for the "indelicacy") is typical of his reasoning.

"and
She *said* thou wast my daughter;"

This subtle touch finds its counterpart in one of Bacon's *Apothegms:*

"There was a young man in Rome that was very like Augustus Caesar: Augustus took knowledge of him, sent for the man, and asked him, 'Was your mother never at Rome?' He answered, 'No, Sir, but my father was.'"

One should note too Colonel Francis Cornwallis Maude, author of *Bacon or Shakspere?* (1895); the prominent German advocate of Bacon, Edwin Bormann, whose *Das Shakespeare-Geheimniss* appeared as *The Shakespeare-Secret* in the same year as Maude's book; and the cautious Edward James Castle (late Lieutenant, Royal Engineers), who in *Shakespeare, Bacon, Jonson and Greene* (1897) argued only that Bacon had helped Shakespeare with some of the plays.

Castle's caution may have been partially induced by the claims of a Detroit physician, Dr. Orville W. Owen, one of the most brilliant researchers in the Delia Bacon–Donnelly tradition, who had in 1893 published the first of five volumes entitled *Sir Francis Bacon's Cipher Story.* Dr. Owen approached the problem of recovering the lost story with scientific skill, inventing (with the help of deciphered instructions from Bacon) and constructing a gigantic machine to aid him. Miss Pruella Janet Sherman, a reporter for the *Detroit Sunday News-Tribune,* has fortunately left us a description of the device as it appeared in 1895.

An immense wheel has been constructed, consisting of two reels, on which is rolled a great stretch of cloth, 1,000 feet long and over two feet wide. The arrangement is so simple that by turning the reel in one direction for a time the entire 1,000 feet of canvas come under the eye, and by reversing the motion all passes back again in the other direction. Upon this stretch of cloth are pasted the printed pages of all the works of all the supposed authors, above mentioned. A more simple or convenient arrangement for examining a great number of pages in a short time could not be devised.

Dr. Owen's machine told an interesting tale, revealing, incidentally, more restraint than Donnelly's key, for it gave to Bacon only his own acknowledged writings plus the works of Shakespeare, Spenser, Greene, Peele, the plays of Marlowe, and Burton's *The Anatomy of Melancholy.* But it also revealed that Bacon was actually the lawful son of Queen Elizabeth, who had been secretly married "by a friar— / A tried holy man" to the Earl of Leicester, and that *Hamlet* had been written as a warning to his mother. There were other bits of Elizabethan lore of the same ilk. All this information was set down by the machine in the from of a long poem somewhat lacking in literary polish, a deficiency for which Owen apologized on behalf of Bacon.

Needless to say, Dr. Owen was subjected to the sneers of the sceptical, and so, like Delia Bacon many years before him, he attempted to locate positive proof of his theories. This time, however, it was not a tomb but a river bed that was pointed to, for his machine had revealed that buried deep in the river Wye were some boxes containing incontrovertible proof of Bacon's authorship and ancestry. Gaining permission from the Duke of Beaufort to excavate, Dr. Owen supervised the digging of eight holes in the banks of the Wye at Chepstowe. Unfortunately, and for reasons which Dr. Owen was apparently never able to determine, the machine had blundered and nothing of literary importance was turned up.

In spite of his final failure, Dr. Owen's labors cannot be said to have been in vain. The machine revealed some astonishing insights to Elizabethan history, and added to the Bacon canon (in addition to the traditional works mentioned above) two new plays, *The Tragical Historie of Our Late Brother Robert, Earl of Essex* and *The Tragedy of Mary Queen of Scots.* If these particular efforts are not quite up to the usual level, their manner of coming to light gives them a unique historical importance. In 1901 Mrs. Elizabeth Wells Gallup, Dr. Owen's co-worker and devoted disciple, extracted a third drama from the assorted texts, publishing it as *The Tragedy of Anne Boleyn.* This play was extracted from Bacon's non-Shakespearean writings by the use of a somewhat modified version of Dr. Owen's cipher method, the details of which had been set forth by her in 1899 in *The Bi-literal Cypher of Sir Francis Bacon,* a volume that went through several editions. Dr. Owen put himself on record as being highly gratified by the achievements of his assistant, Mrs. Gallup, and her assistant, Miss Kate E. Wells.

It is quite fitting to close a chapter on the nineteenth-century adherents of Francis Bacon with Dr. Owen and his disciple Mrs. Gallup. Dr. Owen with his great "WHEEL" was squarely in the most active tradition of the century, the tradition of Delia Bacon and Ignatius Donnelly, the tradition that allowed no historical barrier to stand in its way. Weaned on a cipher and nurtured by an almost mystical reverence for the figure of Bacon, it allowed itself as it grew to claim for its candidate an astonishingly large number of literary pieces, a claim not wholly inconsistent with the highly romantic picture of genius that it attempted to portray. And it was, from the middle of the century to the end, predominantly an American tradition, with W. F. C. Wigston and the later Mrs. Pott the notable exceptions. Further than this it is difficult to generalize, except to observe that the more imaginative theories were not always the work of the literary ladies. Both the legal and the medical mind showed themselves fully at home with the cipher.

The rival tradition, on the other hand, was more truly international, with America, England, and Germany making valuable contributions to its literature. But in their romantic distaste for Shakespeare's humble background, the followers of William Henry Smith and Appleton Morgan conceded nothing to their fellow sceptics. Furthermore, their preference for the genteel Bacon was based upon the same philosophical attitudes as those motivating the cipher hunters. Only in the methods used to demonstrate the validity of their theories did they differ. How important this difference was may be left to the reader to decide.

What must be emphasized, however, is the tremendous popular interest which the Bacon-Shakespeare controversy had created by the last decade of the century. Not only in books, of which those cited in this chapter represent only a small fraction, but in periodicals, newspapers, and from the lecture platform the subject was debated endlessly. It was, without any exaggeration, one of the main topics of discussion among the cultured men and women of the day. Perhaps something of the extent of its appeal can be surmised from the symposium sponsored by the Boston monthly, the *Arena,* in 1892–93. For fifteen months readers were treated to arguments for the plaintiff by Edwin Reed and Ignatius Donnelly; for the defense by the Reverend A. Nicholson, W. J. Rolfe, F. J. Furnivall, and Felix E. Schelling (the last three prominent orthodox scholars); and to verdicts rendered by a jury of twenty-five members, among whom were such distinguished people as Henry George, Edmund Gosse, and Henry Irving. Nor did the fact of the verdicts' being heavily in favor of the man from Stratford in any way diminish the number of sceptics, as the burden of the next chapter will make clear. Indeed, the Baconian heresy kept itself strong, it now appears in retrospect, by means of a loud and anguished opposition from the ranks of faithful Shakespeareans.

Act III

REASON AND LOVE

A Midsummer Night's Dream, III, i

The advent of the twentieth century saw no lessening of the torrent of Baconian books. Such veteran controversialists as Mrs. Gallup, Edwin Reed, and the Honourable R. M. Theobald continued active, but with their ranks reinforced by an impressive array of new converts. In Great Britain the noted jurists, Judge Thomas Ebenezer Webb and the Right Honourable Sir James Plaisted Wilde, Baron Penzance, spoke out, ably seconded by lesser figures like George C. Bompas, Harold Bayley, and the Reverend Walter Begley. More industrious than any of these was Parker Woodward, author of *The Strange Case of Francis Tidir* (1901), who before he was through was to discover Bacon's hand in the works of Shakespeare, Marlowe, Greene, Peele, Jonson, Spenser, Lyly, Nashe, Kyd, Lodge, Gosson, Watson, Puttenham, Burton, and Cervantes. In Germany, too, speculation was rife, with Edwin Bormann retaining his distinction as the Fatherland's greatest Baconian. His *Francis Bacons Reim-Geheimschrift,* translated in 1906 as *Francis Bacon's*

Cryptic Rhymes and the Truth They Reveal, was typical of German scholarship. Possessed of a fine Germanic ear for what he termed Bacon's "curiously rhymed" words, Bormann maintained that hidden rhymes in the *Essays* revealed Bacon's secret. His method of locating these homophonous words is worthy of citation. Discussing the final lines of the fifty-eighth essay, he writes:

Translated into verse, they would run thus:

> But it *is* not *good,*
> to looke too long, upon these turning *Wheeles*
> of Vi*cis*si*tude,*
> lest *we* become Gid*dy.*
> As for th' Philolo*gy*
> of them, that is but a Circle of *Tales.*

"It *is* not *good*" forms a double rhyme to "Vi*cis*si*tude."* "Wheeles"—"Tales" still forms a rhyme to an English ear. The cross-rhymes from one line to the other are delightful. . . .

Perhaps his most brilliant stroke is the identification of Pilate with Shakespeare. When Bacon wrote "What is Truth; said jesting Pilate; And would not stay for an Answer" his real meaning was, according to Bormann, "What is Truth, said the *Actor* Shakespeare . . . 'and would not stay for an answer.' . . . Meaning that the actor, feeling the London pavement growing hot under his feet, had, in the very prime of his manhood, left the City, and retired to the quiet of his native town, Stratford-on-Avon, where he died a few years after." Bormann arrives at this revelation in a relatively simple manner: in Bacon's day to jest meant to play a comic part upon the stage; thus Bacon was really thinking of "the jesting, the acting Pilate!" "But who could that be?" asks the German scholar. And answers:

All we need do is to remember the derivation and meaning of the word "Pilate," "Pilatus" and the question is answered. "Pile" in English, "Pilum" in Latin, is a "spear"; "Pilatus" is one armed

with a "Pilum," a "spear," *i.e.,* a "spear-hurler," a "Lancer,"
"*Shakespeare*."

Bormann represents just a single example of a Teutonic
enthusiasm whose scope can be gauged by the fact that on
at least one occasion a German university actually granted
the doctorate for a Baconian dissertation, a distinction
which, to the best of my knowledge, no American or English university has yet achieved. Nevertheless, the German
interest in Bacon seems to have been largely a derivative
one, and it is necessary to turn back to the English-speaking
countries to find the main currents of the movement. And
there, as in the preceding century, the most imaginative
speculation was taking place in the United States.

A notable contribution was that of Isaac Hull Platt, M.D.,
who demonstrated in *Bacon Cryptograms in Shake-speare,
and Other Studies* (1905) that the letters in "Honorificabilitudinitatibus," a word appearing in a stretch of comic dialogue in *Love's Labour's Lost,* could be rearranged to read
"hi ludi tuiti sibi, Fr. Bacono nati." (As a reward for this
discovery, Platt was allowed to edit *Love's Labour's Lost* for
The Bankside Shakespeare.) In 1909 William Stone Booth
improved upon Platt's orthographical discoveries, demonstrating in *Some Acrostic Signatures of Francis Bacon*
that Jonson's verses opposite the Droeshout portrait of
Shakespeare in the 1623 Folio contained the acrostic signature, "Francis Bacon." The effect of Booth's discovery was
somewhat weakened, however, when Alex. F. Oakey, in a
letter to the *Nation,* claimed the formula also revealed certain Shakespeare sonnets had been written by Isaac Newton,
Robert Browning, Lord Byron, and Theodore Roosevelt.
But by this time a formidable champion had come to
Booth's rescue in a book entitled *Is Shakespeare Dead?*
Surprisingly enough, he published his volume under a pseudonym. Although Samuel Langhorne Clemens' arguments

added nothing essential to the logic of disbelief, they were notable for the colorful language in which they were couched, particularly for the various epithets applied to Shakespeare's supporters, described as "Stratfordolators," "Shakesperoids," "thugs," "bangalores," "troglodytes," "herumfrodites," "blatherskites," "buccaneers," "bandoleers," "muscovites," and, finally, almost despairingly, as "criminals." Henceforth, much of the animus formerly reserved for the Stratford imposter himself was to be directed at his twentieth-century admirers.

In 1910 one of England's most redoubtable warriors entered the lists, by name Sir Edwin Durning-Lawrence, Bart., B.A., LL.B., etc. In *Bacon Is Shake-speare,* Sir Edwin argued that the actor Shakespeare not only could not write his own name, but "was an uneducated rustic, never able to read a single line of print." Unfortunately, Sir Edwin did not dwell upon the possible inconvenience such ignorance could contribute to an actor playing in repertory. But he did tell the reader his reasons for assigning the plays to Bacon. Like Issac Platt, he found proof of his theory in "Honorificabilitudinitatibus," although for him the message was revealed by rearranging the letters to form "HI LUDI F. BACONIS NATI TUITI ORBI." Other clues lay hidden in the 1623 Folio; in the line *"Bome boon for boon prefcian,* a little fcratcht, 'twil ferue"* from *Love's Labour's Lost,* and in the portrait of Shakespeare, in reality "a cunningly drawn cryptographic picture, shewing two left arms and a mask," details unequivocally revealing Bacon as the true author. However, Durning-Lawrence's most elaborate argument was based upon *Gustavi Seleni Cryptomenytices Et Cryptographiae Libri IX. In quibus & planissima Steganographiae a Johanne Trithemio,* a seventeenth-century book on cryptography and stenography. Before he developed his theory, he gave the reader an unusual warning.

If you go to Lunaeburg, where the Cryptographic book was published, you will be referred to the Library at Wolfenbüttel and to a series of letters to be found there which contain instructions to the engraver which seem to prove that this book has no possible reference to Shakespeare. We say, seem to prove, for the writer possesses accurate photographs of all these letters and they really prove exactly the reverse, for they are, to those capable of understanding them, cunningly devised false clues, quite clear and plain. That these letters are snares for the uninitiated, the writer, who possesses a "Baconian" library, could easily prove to any competent scholar.

After this bit of prolegomenon, Sir Edwin proceeded to demonstrate his main thesis that "the great Folio of Shakespeare was published in 1623, and in the following year, 1624, there was brought out a great Cryptographic book by the 'Man in the Moon' . . . issued as the key to the Shakespeare Folio of 1623." Urging his reader to look closely at the facsimile of the title page of this work, he continued:

Examine first the left-hand picture. . . . You see a man, evidently Bacon, giving his writing to a Spearman who is dressed in actor's boots. . . . Note that the Spearman has a sprig of bay in the hat which he holds in his hand. This man is a Shake-Spear, nay he really is a correct portrait of the Stratford house-holder. . . . In the middle distance the man still holding a spear, still being a Shake-Speare, walks with a staff, he is therefore a Wagstaffe. On his back are books—the books of the plays. In the sky is seen an arrow, no, it is not sufficiently long for an arrow, it is a Shotbolt (Shakespeare, Wagstaffe, Shotbolt of Camden's "Remains"). This Shotbolt is near to a bird which seems about to give to it the scroll it carries in its beak. But is it a real bird? No, it has no real claws, its feet are Jove's lightnings, verily, "it is the Eagle of great verse."

Next . . . is the picture on the right of the title page. Here you see that the same Shake-speare whom we saw in the left-hand picture is now riding on a courser. That he is the same man is shewn by the sprig of bay in his hat, but he is no longer a Shake-spear, he is a Shake-*spur*. Note how much the artist has empha-sized the drawing of the spur. It is made the one prominent thing in the whole picture. . . .

Now glance at the top picture on the title page. . . . Note that the picture is enclosed in the magic circle of the imagination, sur-rounded by the masks of Tragedy, Comedy and Farce. . . . The engraving represents a tempest with beacon lights; No; it repre-sents "The Tempest" of Shakespeare and tells you that the play is filled with Bacon lights. (In the sixteenth century Beacon was pronounced Bacon. "Bacon great Beacon of the State.")

At the bottom . . . within the "four square corners of fact," surrounded with disguised masks of Tragedy, Comedy, and Farce, is shewn the same man who gave the scroll to the Spear-man. . . . He is now engaged in writing his book, while an Ac-tor, very much overdressed and wearing a mask something like the accepted mask of Shakespeare, is lifting from the real writer's head a cap known in Heraldry as the "Cap of Maintenance". . . .

Is not this masquerading fellow an actor "Sooping it in his glaring Satten sute"? The figure which we say represents Bacon . . . wears his clothes as a gentleman. Nobody could for a mo-ment imagine that the masked creature . . . was properly wear-ing his own clothes. No, he is "sooping it in his glaring Satten sute."

The whole title page clearly shows that it is drawn to give a revelation about Shakespeare, who might just as well have borne the name of Shotbolt or of Wagstaffe or of Shakespur. . . .

It might not be impertinent to remark at this time that Durning-Lawrence was, according to *Baconiana,* the first person to suspect that Sir Francis Bacon had written *Don Quixote* (a not quite equitable attribution, as an earlier con-tributor to *Baconiana,* one R. P., had in 1896 maintained that Francis Bacon wrote not only the works of Cervantes, but those of Calderón, Lope de Vega, Quevedo, *and* Roger Bacon, the latter because "Francis had to create for himself, not only a public to read his works, but authorities to sup-port them").

Sir Edwin emphasized his arguments by ending key chapters with the legend, "BACON IS SHAKESPEARE," printed in large black type. His assurance did not prevent the appearance four years later of another staunch polemicist, Edward George Harman, Companion of the Bath and Financial Secretary to the Soudan Government under Kitchener of Khartoum. The title of *Edmund Spenser and the Impersonations of Francis Bacon* is revealing of Harman's approach to the problem. Indeed, by the time his posthumous study, *The "Impersonality" of Shakespeare* had appeared in 1925, Harman had added not only Spenser to the Baconian fold, but Lyly, Greene, Nashe, and Sidney, his wholesale appropriations lending a touch of irony to the confession prefixed to his last book that "it will be said that this is more Bacon than Shakespeare; but I cannot distinguish between them."

Meanwhile, on the other side of the Atlantic James Phinney Baxter was also seeking to enlarge the number of Bacon's literary works beyond the mere acquisition of the Shakespeare canon. He looked with favor on the annexation of pieces by Spenser, Peele, Greene, Marlowe, Kyd, and Burton for the busy philosopher. But he was not optimistic about the chances of his theory's meeting with a ready acceptance, for Baxter, sometime mayor of Portland, Maine, and an industrious historian of local Americana, was sunk in gloom as he surveyed Baconian progress to date in *The Greatest of Literary Problems* (1915). The failure of orthodox Shakespeareans to see the light he could explain only on the grounds that they lived in a "delirium" and a "frenzy," having allowed themselves to become "disciples of the new Messianic cult" displaying at Stratford "relics as mythical as the bones of the ten thousand virgins of Cologne, and the pots in which the water was turned to wine at the Galilean marriage feast." When he considered the extent and nature of orthodox literary activity, he was filled with despair, for the praise of Shakespeare's "devotees" would "form a library by itself of forbidding magnitude," yet "if their countervailing opinions were eliminated, the residuum would be inconsiderable, and were the ravings of delirious devotees gathered into a single volume, it would be a curious addition to the library of the alienist."

Baxter's defeatist attitude now appears to have been a bit premature, in view of the celebrated courtroom battle which took place during the following year, the tercentenary of Shakespeare's death. The battle involved, in its legal sense at least, Colonel George Fabyan and William N. Selig. Colonel Fabyan, inspirer of *The Keys for Deciphering the Greatest Work of Sir Francis Bacon* and other similar monographs, was the director of the Riverbank Laboratories of Geneva, Illinois. Strengthened by the presence of Mrs. Elizabeth Wells Gallup, the Laboratories had been conducting an investigation of the Bacon cipher and were preparing publications demonstrating Bacon's authorship of the Shakespearean plays when Selig gained a blocking injunction. Selig, a "motion picture manufacturer," planned to exploit the tercentenary by means of a cinematic tribute to the Bard, and he felt that the publication of the Laboratories' revelations would rather dim the luster of his offer to Shakespeare's memory. The case was heard by Judge Richard S. Tuthill of the Cook County Circuit Court, and his decision made literary, if not legal, history. Here, as reported in the pages of the sedate *Journal of Education* is his verdict.

"That William Shakespeare was born April 23, 1564; that he went to London about 1586 or 1587; that for a time thereafter he made his living working for Burbage; that he later became an actor in Burbage's theatre, and in traveling theatrical companies; that he returned about 1609–1610 to live in Stratford-on-Avon, where he engaged in business to the time of his death, on April 23, 1616, and that Shakespeare was not an educated man, are allegations which the court finds true.

"The court further finds that Francis Bacon was born January 26, 1560 [*sic*]; that he was educated not only in English, but in French, Latin, Italian, German, and had a general education equal or superior to any one of his age; that he was the compiler of a book of 1,560 axioms and phrases selected from the greatest authors and books of all time; that in his youth literary people were frowned upon in England, but in Paris literary people were in the favor of the reigning powers and literature was having a renaissance. Bacon went to Paris in his early youth and spent several years in this atmosphere.

"The court further finds that by the published and accounted works of Francis Bacon there is given a cipher which Bacon devised in his early youth when in Paris, called the Biliteral cipher; that the witness, Elizabeth Wells Gallup, has applied that cipher according to the directions left by Francis Bacon and has found that the name and character of Shakespeare were used as a mask by Francis Bacon to publish facts, stories and statements contributing to the literary renaissance in England which has been the glory of the world.

"The claim of the friends of Francis Bacon that he is the author of said works of Shakespeare, and the facts and circumstances in the real bibliography of the controversy over the question of authority and the proofs submitted herein, convince the court that Francis Bacon is the author."

As concrete evidence of the strength of the court's conviction, Judge Tuthill awarded Colonel Fabyan $5,000 in damages.

The historian must assume that it was the distraction of the war rather than the finality of the judge's verdict (later vacated) that was responsible for the falling off in the number of first-rate Baconian studies in the next few years. By the beginning of the 'twenties, at any rate, activity was on the rise again, and the next ten years were to prove among the most distinguished in the history of the Bacon-Shakespeare controversy. From Germany, by way of translation, came the theories of Dr. Alfred Freund and Amelie Deventer von Kunow. Both Dr. Freund's *The Picture of the Spearshaker:*

The Solution of the Shakespeare Riddle (1921) and Mrs.
von Kunow's *Francis Bacon: Last of the Tudors* (1924)
maintained, on the basis of cryptographic evidence, that Bacon was not only Shakespeare but also the Prince of Wales.
According to her translator, Willard Parker, president of
The Bacon Society of America, "Madame Deventer had
never read any of the other numerous works on the subject,
but plowed the field as absolutely *new ground,*" a position
of scholarly isolation which Parker felt gave to her conclusions "a greatly added weight," so that "no one with an open
mind, or with the slightest cranny therein through which
'revealing day can peep,' can possibly follow Madame Deventer's revelations and remain unconvinced." The English too
were far from idle. Worthy of notice was the lukewarm
Baconian (but red-hot anti-Shakespearean), George Hook-
ham, with his charmingly entitled *Will o' the Wisp, or,
The Elusive Shakespeare* (1922), and the energetic Briga-
dier General S. A. E. Hickson, C.B., D.S.O., author of *The
Prince of Poets and Most Illustrious of Philosophers* (1926).
Dedicated to the mother of Shakespeare, that is, to Queen
Elizabeth, *The Prince of Poets* was "In Memory Of One Of
The Greatest Of Men Who Had No Name Of His Own *
But Who May Be Called By A Whole Library Of Names:
Gascoigne—Laneham—Immerito—Lyly—Broke—Gosson—
Webbe—Puttenham—Watson—Lodge—Daniell—Greene—
Nashe—Peele—Marlowe—Spenser—Cervantes—Montaigne
—Bacon—and Shakespeare." Somewhat more eclectic was
W. Lansdowne Goldsworthy, author of *Shake-speare's
Heraldic Emblems; Their Origin and Meaning* (1928).
Goldsworthy, like Durning-Lawrence a title-page searcher,
is chiefly remembered today for the coyness with which he
asked his readers if Bacon did not "deposit an egg—*Don
Quixote*" and then "another,—*The Journey to Parnassus*—
in the nest of Cervantes?"

In spite of the caliber of the German and British work,
the most imaginative research was again being done in the

United States. From among the many Americans who began their labors during the nineteen-twenties, two, at least,
deserve more than passing notice. First in point of time was
Mrs. Natalie Rice Clark, the author of *Bacon's Dial in
Shakespeare: A Compass-Clock Cipher* (1922). Mrs. Clark,
who could not have written her book without the "steady
cooperation and insistent scholarly method" of her husband,
a professor at Miami University in Ohio, sought to "show
that a cipher designed by Francis Bacon, and based on the
union of a clock and compass in Dial form, exists in the First
Folio of Shakespeare, printed in 1623." With traditional

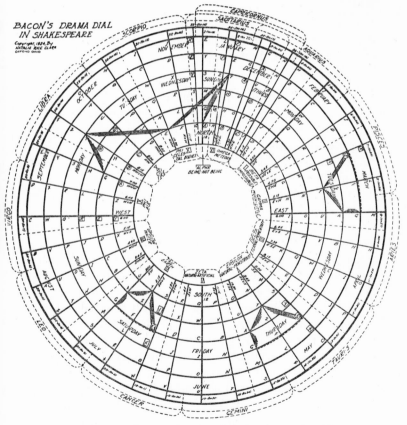

Bacon's Dial Stage, from Natalie Rice Clark, *Hamlet on the Dial Stage*
(Librairie Ancienne Honore Champion, 1931).

caution, Mrs. Clark revealed "only a small portion of the Dial proof," but what was given is almost as difficult to follow as Donnelly's complicated analyses, being presented with an imposing array of diagrams, mazes, and "hour counts," all revealing that "William Shaxberd" was no more than the "pen-man" for the plays. If her conclusions were hardly startling, Mrs. Clark, who found the cipher "a pleasant thing to study, a most sane and human and worthy cipher, both comrade and critic at once," does at least deserve credit for answering a question that had been bothering believers and nonbelievers alike since the days of Delia Bacon. As Mrs. Clark put it: " 'Can a great creative artist limit himself by a haggling cipher?' " Admitting the question to be one of "distinction," she proceeded to answer it, at the same time giving the reader a charming picture of the poet at work.

Every one who writes, whether it is more or less, feels those sudden moments when thought and feeling seem to work from without oneself, and to compel the unexpected presence of unsought words upon the paper. How in such a mood could one pause to insert a word that ought to occur in the ninety-ninth line of the forty-third page of the something cipher?

The reply to this is that Francis Bacon used his Dial cipher exactly as one might use any framework or skeleton of a play. He built his play about it. It was that by which he tried to give balance, harmony, and the sense of living reality.

A poet sometimes takes an intense pleasure in fitting words to a new rhythm, and an artist invents new obligations for himself in the realm of color and line. Bacon, essentially an observer, used his cipher like a note-book or sketch-book. It served to stimulate both his memory and his imagination. He planned his plays to accord with certain harmonizing groups on his Dial-chart. . . .

Bacon's cipher is in the form of a visual guide and is easily memorized. He might have enjoyed using it even if he had been in the forest of Arden, with no chart in the forest. But there was a real "Dial" in the forest. And it is probable that he did in fact work with a real Dial board, on which he moved "pieces" or pegs.

One of the products of Bacon's unique method of Composition was discussed in the volume entitled *Hamlet on the Dial Stage* (1931). The book employs an unusual critical technique, the play being analyzed in terms of puppets moved about on a model stage. But I shall let Mrs. Clark herself explain.

The man who wrote *Hamlet* used in writing and in finishing that play a miniature stage, with miniature figures, or puppets, or cards upon it, as actors. On this toy stage was marked a design, intricate, careful, and yet simple to follow.

The design was formed by a union of clock hours and compass points. The little actors, or cards representing them, travelled around the Dial-marked stage at a rate of progress indicated by the points of the compass. They moved one compass point forward at the end of every speech. The rate of speed was definite, *one speech, one point.*

The clock part of the design was a division of twelve spaces. To each space was given its own peculiar and descriptive title. On the right half, or side, of the Dial each locality was named with rich philosophic meaning: *"Being and Not Being," "Natural and Monstrous," "Natural and Artificial," "Possible and Impossible," "Much and Little," "Eternal and Momentary."* On the left side of the Dial the elements were placed: *"Earth," "Water," "Air," "Fire," "Celestial Bodies,"* and *"Meteors."*

As the actors travelled around the stage, they were made to feel, to think, or to speak under what may be called an "influence" coming from the locality in which they stood at the moment. Thus a certain harmonizing and rhythmical principle was assured from the start, and underlay the whole construction of the play. Recurrences of moods, words, ideas, and actions under the same divisions, or clock-hours, thus affect the reader's mind somewhat as recurrent phrases do in music. This is one explanation of the hold the Shakespeare plays fasten upon the reader.

Moreover, a record was thus kept continuously of all the positions of all the actors in a play, from the first minute to the last. A busy author, leaving his work for awhile, might return and take up his tiny world of people exactly where he left it, accounting for each person, and forgetting none of the minor players. When several dozen characters were involved, as was frequently the case in writing the Shakespeare plays, such a record was valuable to the creator of the mimic world.

There are twenty-nine of these tiny actors upon the Dial stage at the end of *Hamlet*—actors who have distinct speaking parts, not the mutes that may be needed as background. It might trouble any of us in this twentieth century to keep affectionate guard over twenty-nine characters, merely on paper alone. The multitude of actors does give life and human warmth and excitement to the plays, but could not be used without skill and care. The puppet-board, or its equivalent, provided a visible stage on which the play-people became able to take care of themselves quite delightfully.

In rewriting plays from old plots, or in polishing a play again and again, such a device was stimulating and might easily seem invaluable. The device was one that favored collaboration also, since a playwright might readily ask an associate to take up the action at almost any point or to continue the play with a new set of characters. Scenes or parts of scenes might thus be set in like bits of mosaic, and altered or removed at will. In that case, the puppets used by the leading playwright would still dominate the board by their very positions, the other characters having to move around them; and the *"motion"* (as the Elizabethans called a real puppet show) would still continue to be under the guidance of the chief author.

In some of the Comedies the very process of constructing quips and "quiddets" from Dial locations is itself so diverting that one almost believes the playwright must have had a genial partner of two with him at the time of writing. The fun was too good not to be shared with another.

With Mrs. Clark's last sentiment no one can disagree.

As imaginative as Natalie Rice Clark, and better known, was Walter Conrad Arensberg, distinguished Los Angeles art collector and endower of the Francis Bacon Foundation of Pasadena. Arensberg, a lifelong student of cryptography, began his literary investigations in 1921 on an Italian poet, Durante Alighieri, who under another name had written *The Divine Comedy*. In 1922 (having already exposed the true identity of Beatrice in *The Cryptography of Dante*) Arensberg turned to the more fertile field of the Shakespearean plays, publishing *The Cryptography of Shakespeare,* first of several volumes on the subject. Among the more important of these were *The Baconian Keys* (1928) and *The Magic Ring* (1930). While Arensberg had a healthy contempt for historical and stylistic evidence as a basis for determining authorship, he was no admirer of other cryptographers, particularly of Ignatius Donnelly, whom he accused of being "arithmetical." His own system, he emphasized, was orthographical (e.g., the "cross gartered acrostic"), being based on the belief (*cum* Mrs. Pott) that Bacon had founded a secret Rosicrucian society to which he had willed the key to his cipher. Maintaining that this society was still active, functioning within the protecting arms of the Church of England, perhaps even "constituting the *hidden head* of the visible body of the Church," Arensberg accused the then Dean of Lichfield of being a member and of jealously hiding important information from the world, particularly the fact of Bacon and his mother's secret burial in the Lichfield Chapter House. According to Arensberg, members of the society communicated with one another by means of cryptographic messages hidden in the texts of apparently innocent documents such as the easily obtainable tourists' *Hand Guide to Lichfield Cathedral*. The cunning of these prelatical conspirators could nowhere be seen more clearly than in their choice of a hiding place for the secret of Bacon's Lichfield burial, for it was Arensberg's unshakable conviction that this significant information was cryptographically embedded in the seemingly simple wording of the ticket of admission which for six pence admitted tourists to a view of the church at Stratford-on-Avon.

These accusations were made by Arensberg in 1924, in a pamphlet entitled *The Burial of Francis Bacon and His Mother in the Lichfield Chapter House: An Open Communication to the Dean and Chapter of Lichfield Concerning the Rosicrucians.* Arensberg made other charges reflecting upon the Dean's probity. Pointing out that there were secret markings in the Chapter House itself, he noted that "among the signs by which the location of the secret grave in the Lichfield Chapter House has been marked" were "two small stones lying loose in a roughly triangular cleavage between the two slabs which meet, at the location of the chimney at the center of the south wall, in front of the long horizontal grill and immediately above the center of the small perpendicular grill." The importance of these particular stones could not be stressed too much, he felt.

Although I believe that both the cleavages and all the loose stones to which I have referred were intended to be significant, there is a specially important significance which attaches to the cleavage containing the two loose stones. . . . the cleavage was intended as a female symbol, in a sense in which, in accordance with a symbolism which is practically universal, the entrance to the female body and the entrance to the grave are equated; and that the two stones in the cleavage were intended as a male symbol under the guise of a symbolic reference to the Philosopher's Stone, which is traditionally described, in the mystical form of alchemy, as being double in the sense of having two forms and which is to be understood as having an analogue in the male body. In the sense in which I here define the Philosopher's Stone to be understood, there is a reference to the two stones in the cleavage in the following line from *Cymbeline:*

The Stones too hard to come by,

in connection with the wager in accordance with which the stone is to be won; and the same two stones are further to be understood as having a reference to the Masonic symbolism of the stone that was rejected in the building of the Temple and which became the corner stone, in a double sense of corner which signifies (as coign, coin, con) a reference to the female body analogous to the reference in the cleavage, and in a sense which also signifies, by the juxtaposition of the cleavage and the stones, a male and female union.

When, inevitably, the Lichfield authorities swept up the loose stones and cemented over the cleavage, Arensberg had no further doubt about their nefarious motives. Although he immediately challenged "the present members of the Baconian secret society now [to] make a public acknowledgement of the truth which I have spoken as to the secret grave of Francis Bacon and his mother in the Lichfield Chapter House," he was not sanguine of success, for

In view of the fact that the first draft of the present communication, which I have already sent to the Dean and Chapter of Lichfield, has remained unacknowledged, and also in view of the action of the Dean and Chapter in obliterating certain of the signs by which the location of the secret grave was formerly marked and in refusing permission for the taking of photographs which I desired as evidence, I shall not be unprepared if my requests remain unanswered. But whether or not I shall be met, as I have been met in the past, not only by silence but also by denial and by the ridicule which defenders of an established belief find it easy to excite as a weapon of self-defence, I have put the truth on record, and the truth will make its way.

The cryptographical method which leads to Arensberg's discoveries is an interesting one, being described in *The Baconian Keys* as a combination of the compound anagrammatic acrostic, the compound anagrammatic telestic, the Autonymous Master-Key, the Pseudonymous Master-Key, and various Minor Keys, a description replacing the earlier work's "defective definition." The compound anagrammatic telestic is particularly challenging, Arensberg defining it as "a spelling which is intended to represent another spelling." Of interest too is the Pseudonymous Master-Key, the workings of which Arensberg analyzes in the following words: "With no punctuation, WILLIAM SHAKE-SPEARE is added with no punctuation; with ordinary punctuation, a comma follows the name SHAKESPEARE; with periodic punctuation, a period follows each of the two names." One ought not to be surprised that with such tools Arensberg was able to demonstrate that Bacon wrote not only the Shakespearean plays, but parts of the King James version of the Bible as well. Nor that in succeeding years he was able to show that both "Francis Bacon" and "William Shakespeare" were merely pseudonyms of the real author, who was actually William Butts, illegitimate son of Sir William Butts and Lady Anne Cooke Bacon. In addition to his literary and philosophical activities, the talented Butts was heir to the house of Lancaster, and pretender to the throne of England.

Arensberg's energetic, confident publications marked him as one of the most important of Francis Bacon's advocates, as did the large sums of money he spent in the propagation of the faith. It now appears that he deserves another distinction, that of having been the last American supporter of the Elizabethan philosopher to gain a substantial audience. Yet in a sense Arensberg and his contemporary, Mrs. Clark, symbolize the Baconian failure in America. Motivated by a vigorous urban and middle-class dislike for the whole concept of humble rural genius, they sought to create a more pleasing portrait of the artist, one satisfyingly close to the romantic stereotype of the poet, and in each instance it led them to push their theories too far, to extremes that made them seem ridiculous in the eyes not only of orthodox Shakespeareans, but of many staunch heretics. To a certain kind of nineteenth-century mind, the existence of a cipher in the plays was not difficult to understand—belief in it was almost, one might say, a necessity—and the arguments of Delia Bacon, Ignatius Donnelly, and Dr. Owen did not seem illogical. After all, the ways of the Elizabethans were admittedly strange and mysterious. But the theories of Arensberg and Clark were, in a sense, closer to their audience's experience; they were, possibly, too detailed, and the twentieth-century reader found his credulity strained, however much he wanted to believe. It is, one must confess, easier to accept the idea that Bacon was capable of writing seven hundred and eighty plays, than that *Hamlet* was composed by moving puppets round and round a dial. And it is easier to believe that the Elizabethans kept the secret of the authorship, than that the Church of England is at this very moment engaged in Baconian mysteries. Mrs. Clark and Arensberg did, in fact, somewhat overplay their hands, and at a time when the supporters of other candidates were just beginning to demonstrate that cryptography need not be the only arrow to the anti-Shakespearean bow.

The lessening prestige of the Bacon theory in America was soon to be reflected across the sea. For the moment, however, its English proponents seemed to have the situation well in hand. Starting in 1929 and continuing into the early thirties, Bertram Gordon Theobald produced a series of studies, two of which, *Exit Shakespeare* (1931) and *Enter Francis Bacon* (1932), are of interest for their titles if for nothing else. Worthy of mention also is Mr. Roderick Eagle, author of *Shakespeare: New Views For Old* (1930). Mr. Eagle, whose Baconian views were in print by 1916, had read in an ancient account of Edmund Spenser's burial that "he was buried at Westminster, near Chawcer . . . all Poets carrying his body to Church, and casting doeful Verses, and Pens too, into his grave," and he reasoned that Shakespeare, the actor forced to play the role of poet, must have been among those casting verses. Thus if Spenser's grave were to be opened, he argued, a so-called Shakespearean poem would surely be found among the others. The hand, however, would inevitably be Bacon's. In 1938 he managed to get permission to have a look into Spenser's tomb. Unfortunately, Eagle's labors turned up nothing but an old skull and some nondescript bones, and it soon became apparent that he was unable to locate Spenser's actual grave with any certainty. Westminster Abbey authorities, demonstrating a discouraging lack of enthusiasm for the promiscuous excavation of their famous relics, withdrew their coöperation, and, as a result, Mr. Eagle's argument has of necessity remained confined to the realm of theory.

Among other scholars of the period should be noted John Denham Parsons and A. B. Cornwall. Parsons, who in 1927 had published *Non-Partisan Shakespeare Decipherings,* soon dispensed with the handicap of objectivity and between 1930 and 1935 wrote a series of polemical volumes on the Baconian cipher, volumes containing, in the words of another dissenter, "unassailable" discoveries, "authenticated by the highest English authorities on the calculus of probabilities." He was followed in 1936 by A. B. Cornwall, a certified public accountant, whose *Francis the First, Unacknowledged King of Great Britain and Ireland, Known to the World as Sir Francis Bacon, Man of Mystery and Cipher,* advanced the familiar thesis that Queen Elizabeth's impenetrable virginity was a legendary thing. More impressive than that of either Parsons or Cornwall was the work of Alfred Dodd, a dissenter whose publications appear to have had somewhat the same effect on British Baconian activity that Arensberg's had earlier exerted on American. Dodd began in a modest manner in 1931 with an edition of the Shakespeare sonnets entitled *The Personal Poems of Francis Bacon (Our Shake-speare) the Son of Queen Elizabeth,* rearranging the sonnets so that they told a lively Baconian story, a story exciting enough to provoke numerous editions in the next few years. Something of its wide appeal can be gained from the concluding pages of the sixth edition (1938) which the present writer has before him. Appended to the little volume is a long list of commendatory comments sent to Dodd by admirers of the earlier editions. Each opinion is prefaced by the name and occupation (author, journalist, lawyer, and so forth) of its writer. The following, purporting to be a letter from a Mr. Austin, is given in its entirety:

Mr. AUSTIN. *a Working Man:* I have never had much time for reading—especially poetry, but I did not find the Sonnets difficult to understand. It is quite a straight story. It gripped me and instructed me. It has made me change my opinions because it sounds true. I would like to see the Life Story of the Author on the Films. It would make a grand Picture.

Buoyed by this plebeian panegyric, Alfred Dodd set to work in earnest, soon becoming one of the most prolific of Bacon's advocates. His growing confidence and perception are succinctly illustrated by the informative titles of his books, representative examples of which are given below:

Shakespeare, Creator of Freemasonry; Being a Remarkable Examination of The Plays and Poems, Which Proves Incontestably That These Works Were Saturated in Masonry, That Shakespeare Was A Freemason and The Founder of The Fraternity, 1937.

The Marriage of Elizabeth Tudor; Being An Exhaustive Inquiry into Her Alleged Marriage with The Earl of Leicester and The Alleged Birth of Her Two Sons, Francis Bacon and The Earl Of Essex: An Historical Research Based on One of The Themes in "Shakespeare's Sonnets," 1940.

The Secret Shake-speare; Being The Missing Chapter from "Shakespeare, Creator of Freemasonry" in Which The Identity Of Shake-speare Is Plainly Declared, Together With Many Curious Secret Messages of Profound Interest to All Lovers of Literature, to Elizabethan Students and Freemasons in Particular, 1941.

The Immortal Master, by Alfred Dodd; Being A Study of The
Greatest Genius of The English-speaking Race, The Creator of
The English Renaissance, "Shake-speare," from A New Angle in
The Knowledge That He Possessed an Experimental Familiarity
with The Supernormal Hitherto Unsuspected, with Some Re-
markable Evidence Indicating His Interest Today in "This Royal
Throne of Kings, His [!] Sceptr'd Isle, This Earth of Majesty,
This Seat of Mars, This Other Eden, Demi-Paradise," 1943.

Alfred Dodd's belief that the plays and poems were "Saturated in Masonry" found ready acceptance from a young
Californian, Mrs. Maria Bauer, author of *Francis Bacon's
Great Virginia Vault* (1939) and *Foundations Unearthed*
(1940). Mrs. Bauer not only argued that "Lord Bacon" was
the founder of Freemasonry, but also that *"The Constitution of the United States,* and the main course of its History,
were predetermined and carried out in accordance with Sir
Francis Bacon's plan of Empire-building," an argument that
makes questions of literary authorship appear of somewhat
limited significance (actually Bacon was the "guiding genius" behind the plays: among his co-authors were Lancelot
"Andrews," "Toby Mathews," John Donne, Ben Jonson,
Edmund "Spencer," Sir Walter Raleigh, George "Withers,"
and "many others" including Sir Francis Drake). Documents revealing Bacon's manifold activities, of which the
writing of plays was but one small part, were brought to
Jamestown, Virginia, in 1653, and now lie buried in the
"Bruton Vault" at Williamsburg, according to Mrs. Bauer.
The young lady actually received permission to engage in
the traditional excavatory activities, but the Williamsburg
authorities soon became disillusioned (or, in Mrs. Bauer's
eyes, "motivated by ill will" to suppress "a constructive and
immeasurably beneficent work") and her labors were of
necessity terminated. Still convinced that Bacon's master
plan for humanity lay deep in the Virginia earth, Mrs.

Bauer closed *Foundations Unearthed* with a moving appeal to her countrymen:

America—cast your vote for the salvation of your own Future, for the recognition of your great Founder, the empire-builder of your Nation and your Culture, the giver of the most stupendous "God-father-gift" ever prepared for Man—the Hope and Salvation of your oppressed misguided Brothers in Europe. File your claim for the uncovering of Bruton Vault, so that the fruits of this tremendous work may yield a healing medicine for the sick earth—a work which is enduring, because it is founded upon the very gravity-point of nature, is anchored in the Soul of the Human race, recorded in the fraternal ideal of world-wide organizations, reflected in the eyes of a young Nation, chronicled in the secret records of the human elect, audible in the living text of immortal writings,—a voice growing into song, absorbing the wails of a war-ridden world, destined to merge into a glorious symphony heralding the Birth of a New Age, the time of Man's coming into his great Inheritance, because his truly royal birth and spiritual destiny, his claim to true HUMANITY has been recognized.

The reader will already have noted certain similarities between Maria Bauer and her predecessor, Delia Bacon. Indeed, in her enraptured appreciation of the wisdom and genius of the great philosopher, Mrs. Bauer concedes nothing to Bacon's earlier admirer, and insofar as opening tombs is concerned, she reveals little of her prototype's necrophobic timidity. Delia Bacon, of course, retreated into insanity after her failure to open the grave at Stratford. The writer of this history regrets that he does not know what became of Mrs. Bauer after her similar failure. All he can report is that by 1948, according to information pasted to the title page of the third printing of *Foundations Unearthed,* she was on the staff of the "First Temple and College of Astrology," located in Los Angeles, and holding classes on Tuesdays and Thursdays. It has also been recorded that she eventually remarried and became the wife of the mystic, Manly P. Hall.

The recent history of the Baconian movement has been marked by a noticeable falling off in the number, if not in the quality, of partisan publications. To what extent the decline results from the challenge of other candidates rather than the Baconians' own enthusiasm is difficult to tell. Whatever the cause, the decline does not mean that the Bacon-Shakespeare controversy is in the process of dying down completely. The Bacon Society is still active in England, still publishing *Baconiana,* and a regular, if small, stream of books and pamphlets still flows from the presses. Alfred Dodd, Edward D. Johnson, Howard Bridgewater, Kate Prescott, and H. Grute, to name but a few, have all published books since the last war. Perhaps the most important recent student, a forerunner of the new conservatism characteristic of many British Baconians, was William Stanley Melsome, M.D., editor of *Baconiana* and president of The Bacon Society until his death in 1944. "In his time he was a fine cricketer, being invited by J. E. K. Studd (Sir Kynaston Studd) in 1884 to play for the University" writes Roderick Eagle. He was also the author of "numerous medical works, particularly on Anatomy." Not surprisingly, his contribution to the cause consisted of a book entitled *The Bacon-Shakespeare Anatomy* (1945). Dr. Melsome's study is an "investigation and observation of the resemblances and analogies between the work of Bacon and of Shakespeare" (such as their both using the expression, to knit the brows) and is squarely in the sober tradition of William Henry Smith. Its conservative tone made it an important step in the direction of regaining some of the Baconian movement's lost prestige.

In a quite different vein is the work of a gentleman from Indiana, whose claims are of a nature to warrant our notice even though they were not published in book form. In January, 1956, the *Indianapolis Star* ran a series of articles on the disclosures of William L. Gaines, Hoosier magazine editor and cryptologist. Maintaining (not surprisingly) that Bacon had entered into a secret agreement with William Shakespeare for the use of the latter's name, Gaines brings to light some fascinating items of forgotten history. In addition to the oft-suspected fact that Bacon was Elizabeth's son, he reveals that Shakespeare died of a venereal disease and that his body was taken from its tomb and thrown into the Avon, a lead urn containing evidence of the secret agreement being substituted in its place. But the Indianan's most important contribution to history is his enlargement of the Bacon canon, a harvest impressive even by Baconian standards. In addition to the Shakespearean poems and plays, Gaines claims for Bacon all the works of Spenser, Marlowe, and Milton, as well as *Pilgrim's Progress,* "Elegy Written in a Country Churchyard," *The Compleat Angler,* Montaigne's *Essais,* Bryant's "Thanatopsis," and Poe's poems, "The Raven" and "Lenore" (the last, rather interestingly, having been written for Queen Margaret of Navarre, with whom Bacon had fallen in love at the age of eighteen). Gaines completes his list by awarding the philosopher Rose Hartwick Thorpe's "Curfew Shall [*sic*] Not Ring Tonight," and by revealing that he was the editor of the Authorized Version of the Bible (a task undertaken as a personal favor for King James). Gaines also discloses that Bacon invented the steam engine, weaving a secret account of the invention into the Shakespearean poem, *Venus and Adonis.* Detailed evidence of these historical facts is hidden in secret caches in England, says Gaines, who knows their location but does not wish to reveal it until he is sure of obtaining "some modest award" for his many years of labor in breaking the Baconian code.

Mr. Gaines, whom the *Indianapolis Star* describes as hurling the "serious charge" of "Fraud!" at "the Titians [*sic*] of English literature," admits that his methods of investigation are based on the cipher theories of Ignatius Donnelly. But he avers that he has made great improvements on Donnelly, whom he accuses of being "erratic and full of errors." Donnelly, says Gaines, was "on the right train but on the wrong track." Yet actually Gaines' methods appear to differ little from his forerunner's, while of his historical disclosures only the enlargement of the Baconian canon offers anything essentially new. One feels that though in a symbolical sense Gaines may mark a fitting conclusion to a history of the Baconian movement, it would be unwise to take him and his discoveries too seriously.

Between the modest claims of the Reverend Mr. Wilmot and the more sweeping assertions of Mr. Gaines stretches a vast body of polemical literature designed to persuade the world that William Shakespeare was a fraud. The number of books and articles and newspaper accounts defies discussion (over thirty years ago one dissenter claimed that he had read some five thousand works on the subject), but one fact is clear; until recent years most of them were Baconian in character. From the authors of this astonishing body of writings, it has been possible here to catalogue only a few of the more energetic and serious advocates of the great Elizabethan philosopher. We have had to ignore such eccentrics as those people who in the 1920's argued that Bacon was still alive in some pleasant English manor house, writing great works soon to be revealed to the world; the clairvoyant lady who sailed round and round the Bermudas, seeking the cave wherein Bacon had hidden the manuscripts of the plays when, disguised as a woman, he had made a hurried trip to the islands to find a place in which to protect his works from the breath of scandal; and J. Edward Morgan of Alameda, California, who believed that Bacon was not only Shakespeare, but Edward VI too. Nor have we had an opportunity to elaborate upon such biographical discoveries as Bacon's confession that he poisoned Shakespeare;

the claim that Bacon was a hermaphrodite; or the Juliet-like trip across the Channel when Bacon, rendered temporarily dead by a hypnotic drug of his own devising, was stuffed into a barrel, smuggled to safety, and then revived by an injection he himself had previously prepared.

Overlooked too have been Peter Alvor (Burkhard Herrman), who in *Die Shakespeare-Frage und das Ben Jonson-Problem* (1930) took the unusual stand that Bacon wrote Jonson's plays but not Shakespeare's, and the many examples of formal imaginative literature inspired by the claims made on Bacon's behalf. Among this literature have been historical romances like Climenson Yelverton Charles Dawbarn's *Uncrowned* (1913), and an impressive number of dramas. William R. Leigh's *Clipt Wings, A Drama in Five Acts, Being an Explanation of the Mystery Concerning the Authorship of the Works Attributed to Shakespeare, the Parentage of Francis Bacon, and the Character of Shaxper* (1930), and Wallace McCook Cunningham's *The Tragedy of Francis Bacon, Prince of England* (1940) are typical of the latter. Atypical, even for the history of the Baconian movement, is Philip Francis Samuels' *Man v'ape in the play Ear—ce—rammed,* the purpose of which is to "assert that Jesus, Bacon and P. Samuels, is one and the same man."

If sheer weight of evidence could decide a question, then undoubtedly Sir Francis Bacon, onetime Baron Verulam, Viscount St. Alban, and Lord Chancellor of England, would have to be awarded the bays. He has not been; and ironically the failure may be due in the last analysis to one of his stoutest champions, for it was Ignatius Donnelly who wrote that "in all ages it has been the multitude who were wrong, and the few who were right." With the Baconians doomed by their very success, small wonder that wise men turned their attention to other candidates whose claims to be The Author could not be damaged by a quick and ready acceptance.

Act IV

BY BUD OF NOBLER RACE

Winter's Tale, IV, iv

It will be useful at this time to attempt to reach a few conclusions about the nature of the Bacon-Shakespeare controversy. Perhaps its most striking characteristic has been that
of personal emotion. The typical supporter of Bacon has not
been an objective investigator, laboring with the sole purpose of uncovering historical truths, whatever they might
turn out to be. He has been, rather, a crusader, struggling
with high religious fervor to right the wrong done to his
man. Convinced that there exists among orthodox admirers
of Shakespeare's works an organized conspiracy to maintain
the legend of the Stratford imposter, he has tended to release
his frustrations not only upon the conspirators, but upon the
passive figures of Shakespeare and Bacon. Toward Shakespeare, the result has usually been a strong and bitter hatred;
toward Bacon, a burning mystical worship, the flames
fanned by the conviction that history has done the philosopher a great injustice. For reasons that a sociologist could
probably explain, the social differences between the Strat-

94

ford man and the Elizabethan courtier have been a critical factor in creating and prolonging the emotional turbulence that the Baconian has typically suffered.

Originated (for practicable purposes) by Victorians of the last century, and kept alive largely by Victorians of this one, the Baconian argument has been strongly marked by efforts at imaginative reconstruction. Gradually the claims made on the philosopher's behalf were pushed further and further, a symptom related, perhaps, to the world's failure to be convinced of the truth of the basic premise. To some people it began to appear that the supporters of Bacon were interested not so much in proving that he had written the plays, as in creating a kind of Olympian mythology around him. It was time, said the more scientifically minded among the Shakespearean dissenters, to come down to earth. The theories to be discussed in the present chapter are to a great extent attempts to do just that, to leave the realm of Baconian fantasy for the world of modern historical investigation—scientific, reasonable, detached.

It will be recalled that while a few people, such as Appleton Morgan and Thomas W. White, had refused to put both feet on the Bacon bandwagon, most nineteenth-century writers had built their case against Shakespeare solely on the basis of their claims for the Elizabethan scientist. There had been other exceptions, notably Jesse Johnson, who in *Testimony of the Sonnets as to the Authorship of the Shakespearean Plays and Poems* (1899) had argued, without advancing a substitute author, that Shakespeare could not have written the sonnets and the poetic passages of the great dramas. But these aberrations had not disturbed the Baconian confidence, based on the solid entrenchment of rank upon rank of the faithful. However, as the new century dawned, the defenses of Bacon's adherents were struck a damaging blow, just how damaging no one at the time quite realized. It was delivered by the noted American naturalist,

William H. Edwards, author of *The Butterflies of North America*. In 1900 Edwards published a volume entitled *Shaksper Not Shakespeare,* in which he retraversed the argument that unorthodoxy was by now taking more or less for granted; that is, that William Shakespeare of Stratford-on-Avon could not by any stretch of the imagination have written the plays. Edwards demonstrated the validity of his thesis in considerable detail, even if the detail itself was not noticeably new.

It is full time that reasonable men should re-examine the evidences on which they have believed that an illiterate butcher, from an ignorant and bookless inland village, who flew to London in disgrace before the constable, and became a servitor, and later, a player at a public theater, the then most degraded place of amusement, and who spent the greater part of every year in strolling through England with his troupe of comedians, sat himself down, and without preparation or knowledge, dashed off Hamlet,—and not only Hamlet, but nearly two score of the world's greatest plays.

While Edwards is important for reëmphasizing the negative argument, his real contribution lies in the fact that he refused to state who had written the controversial plays, restricting himself to the suggestion that a wise move would be to look over the Elizabethan scene more carefully.

I would suggest that searchlights be turned on the judicious Hooker, or the worthy Donne, or the learned Coke, or Tobie Matthew, or Lord Burleigh himself. One and all apparently had the habit of writing and the trick of expression.

Or, if these names are not satisfactory, give a thought to the many acknowledged play-writers of that age, university men, who wrote singly or in collaboration—Daniel, Marlowe, Greene, and the rest.

Edwards' failure to mention Bacon among his likely candidates revealed the flaw that was soon to split the army of dissent into numerous warring groups. Not only had he shown that it was possible to ignore the long shadow of Francis Bacon, but he had tendered an invitation that was to prove irresistible to countless admirers of the disputed literature. To a small minority it was the former point that was significant, the demonstration that one could doubt Shakespeare without having to accept the unpoetic, bribe-tainted Elizabethan lawyer in his place. By far the most important of these upholders of the negative proposition was the eminent barrister, Sir George Greenwood, K.C., M.P., author during the first three decades of the century of numerous books designed merely to show that Shakespeare the Player and Shakespeare the Poet were not the same person. Representative of his efforts are *The Shakespeare Problem Restated* (1908) and *Is There A Shakespeare Problem?* (1916), sizable volumes crammed with learned details of Elizabethan lore, written in a style ornately graceful and judicial. Leavening almost every page was a sharp and penetrating wit, and if Sir George's writing was lacking in the heavy invective disfiguring the manifestoes of many of his fellow dissenters, it was nevertheless capable of flashes of sophisticated cruelty worthy of a Rochester or a Pope. Typical is his dismissal of Churton Collins and Sidney Lee (not yet Sir Sidney), two mighty orthodoxians with whom Greenwood had frequently clashed. Lee, in particular, had been, and was to continue to be, harsh on nontraditionalists, visiting anathemas upon their heads in much the same language that the heretics were accustomed to apply to Stratfordians. Pointedly relegating the whole discussion to the small print of a footnote, Sir George wrote:

Messrs. Sidney Lee and Churton Collins are, of course, distinguished in the realms of literature and criticism, and I trust I shall always write of them with becoming respect. They speak, it seems, with authority, and not as the scribes, and no doubt feel that they are entitled to hurl thunderbolts from their high altitudes on the heads of lowlier mortals who are so presumptuous as to disagree with them, although they not infrequently disagree as between themselves. It is not unnatural to inquire who those are who take upon themselves to chastise us with scorpions, and the historian of criticism will note of these "duo fulmina belli" that they are both men of Balliol, and, by a rather curious coincidence, both took a Second Class Degree in Modern History, Mr. Collins in 1872, and Mr. Lee, just ten years afterwards. To be strictly accurate Mr. J. C. Collins, as we learn by the Oxford Calendar of 1873 (p. 148), took his B.A. degree, in 1872, with a Second Class "In Jurisprudentia et Historia Moderna," i.e. in "Law and Modern History"; while Mr. Lee, as appears from the Calendar of 1883 (p. 54), took his B.A., in 1882, with a Second Class "In Historia Moderna," Jurisprudence having by that time been separated from Modern History. In the Calendar of 1880 he is mentioned for the first time as Minor Exhibitioner of Balliol College. For the benefit of the puzzled investigator (and such, at first, was I) it may be mentioned that he there appears under a slightly different form of appellation to that by which he is now familiar to us, not having at that date discarded two Biblical *praenomina* in order to assume the more Saxon name of Sidney. I cannot help thinking, by the way, that Mr. Sidney Lee might be rather more tolerant of those who imagine that some great man in Elizabethan times might have seen advantages in the assumption of a pseudonym.

Sir George's efforts provoked that rarest of accolades for the nonbeliever, serious full-length attempts at rebuttal from the pens of well-known traditionalist scholars. Among his disputants were such men of letters as H. C. Beeching, Andrew Lang, and J. M. Robertson, to whose published criticism Sir George replied in further learned volumes. Yet for all his vast knowledge and reasonable, judicial tone, his basic thesis varied not at all from that of his more splenetic predecessor, Edwards. Unlike Edwards, he failed to inspire any follower of note, and it would appear that arguing against Shakespeare without identifying oneself with a rival candidate has small appeal. The American, William Leavitt Stoddard ("M.A., Harvard"), attacked the Stratford legend without advancing a candidate in *The Life of William Shakespeare Expurgated* in 1910, but his failure to come out and name Bacon explicitly was primarily an attempt to lend an air of objectivity to his work; the careful reader could have had no difficulty in guessing that Stoddard's heart was with the philosopher all the time. Somewhat nearer to Greenwood was William H. Chapman whose *William Shakspere and Robert Greene. The Evidence* (1912) presents the negative case, but in a violently unreasonable manner. Worthy of note, too, is Joseph Martin Feely, who in *Deciphering Shakespeare* (1934) and subsequent studies combined the arguments of Greenwood and Donnelly to create a wild and startling tale concerning the unnamed author of the plays, a tale so risqué, incidentally, that the decipherer did not dare reveal the "intimé items in these secret memoirs." But with few exceptions, the man who is against Shakespeare has had inevitably to be for someone else.

The importance of Edwards and Greenwood, therefore, lies in the sanction they gave to the desertion of Francis Bacon. One result of this sanction—and a relatively minor one—was the attempt to revive the group theory of Delia Bacon. As early as 1904 Judge John Stotsenburg of Indiana had accepted Edward's invitation to turn the searchlights on the "acknowledged play-writers of that age" and in *An Impartial Study of the Shakespeare Title* decided that the plays had been written by a group composed of Drayton, Dekker, Heywood, Webster, Middleton, Porter, Munday, and Chettle (John Fletcher may have had a hand in them too). Relegated to an irritatingly minor role was Bacon, given credit for some revisions to *Hamlet*. In 1928 the group theory was again revived, this time by Ernest A. Gerrard, who in *Elizabethan Drama and Dramatists 1583–1603* held that the plays were products of a group including Lyly, Marlowe, Kyd, Peele, Greene, Nashe, Drayton, Dekker, and Chettle.

An arresting feature of Gerrard's theory was the role al-
lotted to Shakespeare, described as a mere reviser and pretty
much of a botcher at that—even in *Hamlet* "he still lacks
all understanding of true dramatic construction, of dramatic
unity. Like a jobbing mason he still patches bit to bit." The
next "Groupist," noticeably more aristocratic in outlook,
was the eminent historian and economist, Dr. Gilbert Slater,
who in *Seven Shakespeares* (1931) maintained that the plays
were the work of Derby, Marlowe, Rutland, Oxford, Raleigh,
the Countess of Pembroke, and, in a minor role again,
Bacon. It has been held, perhaps unjustifiably so, that Dr.
Slater included Bacon only because he wanted to get into his
book all the popular candidates of the moment. One of the
most notable features of his volume is the supreme confidence
with which he apportions the Shakespearean plays among
his various candidates, reserving, with a happy touch of gal-
lantry, large parts of the romantic comedies for the lady.

Actually the group theory has never been a popular one,
probably because it is not much more satisfying to owe allegiance to a multitude of candidates than to none at all. It
was inevitable, therefore, that many of the people to whom
the name of Shakespeare was anathema should start looking
over the Elizabethan landscape in search of a single ideal
figure on whom they could pin their hopes, once it had been
demonstrated that belief in Sir Francis Bacon was not a
necessary condition of disbelief in William Shakespeare. As
a result of this search, a goodly number of Elizabethan per-
sonalities have been exhumed, cleaned up, and put on public
display, each one with appropriate affidavits assuring us
that his appearance is the result of modern methods of research and not of Baconian whimsy. With very few exceptions these resurrected Elizabethans have one important
attribute in common—whatever their other qualifications
for the great honor may or may not be, they are represented
as creatures of reassuringly gentle breeding, sophisticated

courtiers to a man, a phenomenon that the reader, at this stage of our narrative, may not find wholly unanticipated. Of this galaxy of knights and noblemen, three names stand out, if only because each has attracted the support of enough backers to have remained in contention over a significant period of time.

First to have his claims made known was William Stanley, sixth Earl of Derby, whose resurrection, although largely accomplished during the present century, was first proposed at the end of the nineteenth. His initial sponsor was a British archivist, James Greenstreet, who published in the years 1891–1892 three essays detailing his discovery of two sixteenth-century letters which mentioned that the Earl of Derby was busy writing comedies for the common players. Filled with the traditional distaste for the idea of a low-born author, Greenstreet found his discovery cause enough to suggest the Earl as a substitute for Shakespeare. Unfortunately, Greenstreet died after completing his third essay, and without Edwards' subsequent extra-Baconian arguments to lend force to his beliefs, his remarkable theories were neglected (except for T. U. D.'s attempt to exploit them in *Baconiana* in 1897) for almost twenty-five years. It was an American, Robert Frazer, who revived the Derby theory, arguing in *The Silent Shakespeare* (1915) that although Shakespeare "popularised" (i.e., vulgarized) old plays, he could not have written the magic lines of the disputed dramas. On the other hand, one "plausibly answers the question 'Who was Shakespeare?' by replying; William Stanley was William Shakespeare."

For some reason, Frazer's advocacy of Derby has been completely overlooked, and a French scholar, Abel Lefranc, has been awarded the mantle as Derby's first modern supporter. Lefranc, Professeur de la Collège de France, and well known as a writer on Rabelais and the French Renaissance, expanded Greenstreet's original arguments in *Sous le*

Masque de William Shakespeare: William Stanley, VIe *comte de Derby,* an impressive two-volume study of the problem, published in 1919. He reaffirmed his position four years later in *Le Secret de William Stanley* and again in 1945 in *À la Découvert de Shakespeare.* M. Lefranc, whose theory is based upon similarities he discovered between scenes and characters in a handful of Shakespeare's plays and key events of Derby's life, stressed that the attitudes expressed in the plays are those of an aristocrat: "c'est un membre d'une aristocratie qui parle et qui traite les chose en noble éclairé avec les conceptions propres aux membres des classes dirigeantes." Therefore, the works published under the name of "l'acteur William Shakespeare" could not possibly "avoir été composés par ce personnage." Lefranc was particularly struck by the courtly tone of the comedy, *Peines d'Amour perdues,* a play which had once, it may be recalled, made the Reverend Mr. Wilmot turn unhesitatingly to Bacon.

The theories of Lefranc received instant support from Jacques Boulenger, who defended them in *L'Affaire Shakespeare,* also published in 1919, and the Derby hypothesis has enjoyed a certain favor ever since. During the twenties and thirties numerous articles by Lefranc helped keep the theory alive, and in 1937 the Derby cause was joined by Richard Macdonald Lucas, author of *Shakespeare's Vital Secret (Known to His Queen).* In 1938 Mathias Morhardt brought forth *A la rencontre de "William Shakespeare,"* with a preface by Lefranc; the following year A. W. Titherley published *Shakespeare's Sonnets as from the Pen of William Stanley, Sixth Earl of Derby.* Dr. Titherley is certainly one of the most unlikely polemicists in the whole history of Shakespearean scepticism. A distinguished chemist and formerly Dean of the Faculty of Science at the University of Liverpool, he attempted in *Shakespeare's Identity* (1952) to apply the "scientific method" and its formulae to the solution of the problem, promising to reason "partly by deduc-

The printer or compositor tried more faithfully to reproduce the spelling before him than the scrivener, and H. C. Wyld said (*History of modern colloquial English*, p. 112) " printers are unlikely to introduce, of themselves, any considerable novelties in spelling." This is generally true of reprinting from printed texts (as shown by successive editions of the Quartos), unless reprinted much later ; but compositors, though to a less degree than scriveners, also reduced the number of y-spellings when printing from manuscripts, and fairly consistent results in general calculations are obtained if it is assumed that they cancelled out on average nearly half such y-spellings, so as to give a reduction factor f_p of about ·54.

The empiric formulae, which have been thus derived, with some uncertainty as to the magnitude of the constants, are :—

Index of author $I_a = 100 \cdot e^{(\cdot 06 x_a - \cdot 068 y_a)}$ .... (2)

Scrivener's reduction factor $f_c = \dfrac{x_c}{3 x_{a_1}}$ .... (3)

Printer's reduction factor $f_p = \cdot 54$ .... (4)

Scrivener's Index $I_c = I_a \times f_c$ .... (5)

Printer's Index $I_p = \cdot 54 I_c$ (if printed from a copy) .... (6)

$I_p = \cdot 54 I_a$ (if printed from autograph) .... (7)

where I_a, I_c and I_p = frequency Index, as defined above, respectively of autograph, copy or printed text, and

x_a = age of author at the time of writing ; x_{a_1} = his age at the time of copying ;

x_c = age of scrivener at the time of copying ;

y_a = date of author's autograph minus 1550.

These related expressions (*hereinafter called the ' standard equations '*) roughly fit the facts where known, but they are valid only for writers, scriveners or compositors born after 1550, and since they take no cognisance of unknown personal factors they are necessarily only approximate. Any attempts to find ideal formulae which would cover all dates and persons, even if possible, would introduce such complexity as to make mathematical analysis merely picturesque but useless ; and all that can be claimed for the new method is that, in spite of its limitations, it offers a serviceable means of settling a number of disputed questions concerning Shakespeare and indeed other writers of the period. As the ages of different authors are generally known, also usually the date of writing and printing, but not the ages of scriveners, solution of the standard equations is only possible by trying out different assumed ages for the latter ; and those solutions are accepted as in general satisfactory, which would require that x_c should lie between 20 and 40. In this way the formulae set limits within which it is often possible to deduce whether a given text was printed direct from autograph or from a copy, and if the latter to arrive at the Index I_a of the author through equations (3) to (7), quite independently of (2), namely by finding what figure will inductively satisfy the varying observed I_p values of widely different samples of his text.

Shakespeare's theoretical handwriting Index, I_a, calculated from equation (2) for 1590, comes out at nearly 40, assuming that his age, x_a, was then 30, but it should be noticed that such calculated values for different writers are dependent on the fixed constants in (2), constants however which are not arbitrary in the case of Shakespeare because they have been determined by many observations of y-spellings scattered through the 1623 Folio. But canonical Quarto I_p values are sometimes so low as to suggest that where this is the case they were printed from *copies of copies*, which would of course be beyond the scope of the standard equations.

An important question at once arises concerning the actual *distribution* of y-spellings in any piece of text or autograph. Though the overall frequency of any writer was virtually constant, in practice when writing he did not spin out his y-spellings evenly but purely as a matter of chance, so that over (say) any ten consecutive lines there might be found sometimes

Page showing typical formula, from A. W. Titherley, *Shakespeare's Identity*

(Warren and Son, 1952).

tion but mainly by induction." He proposed, if a layman can presume to understand his admittedly complex ratiocination, to destroy the Shakespeare myth by the inductive method alone. In discovering the true author, however, a bit of deduction seems to be permissible, for Dr. Titherley felt it was not unscientific to assume a necessary condition, a condition which he described as the author's "literary sincerity." "Literary sincerity among other things denotes the expression of a writer's own perception, without any pretence to a first hand knowledge which is second hand, and Shakespeare certainly betrays such realistic fidelity to truth in so many ways that it is exceedingly probable (to put it mildly) that he had experienced many of these things." From this condition, one could "lay down certain prerequisites which must be fulfilled" by the candidate; for instance, that he had the "Christian name William" and "was intimate with the English and foreign courts." These "prerequisite inferences" were not "mere didactic statements of opinion, because they flow logically from what Shakespeare has written, if realistic sincerity denotes first hand experience, for then the latter serves as a binding mediate term in each underlying syllogism." At this point Dr. Titherley gives the reader an example of his syllogistic reasoning.

(i) Shakespeare wrote with realistic sincerity about courts of all kinds; (ii) such sincerity, as defined, always connotes first hand knowledge; (iii) therefore he was intimate with these courts.

And therefore, he must have been a courtier, of which none was more so than the Earl of Derby. This from the former Dean of the Faculty of Science at the University of Liverpool.

Dr. Titherley found an ardent disciple four years later in Mr. A. J. Evans, author of *Who's The Guy* and *The V-2 Expert*. Evans' admiration for the learned doctor pulsates on almost every page of *Shakespeare's Magic Circle* and is matched only by his absolutely awesome admiration for the aristocracy. Seldom, indeed, has sensitivity to social stratification been more keenly developed than by Mr. Evans. As a consequence, he can dismiss the Stratford actor with what is, even for this history, unusual dispatch: "there is no avoiding the conclusion that Shakespeare [i.e., the real author] was an aristocrat—it is self-evident." Actually one aristocrat is hardly enough for Evans, and his affinity for blue blood makes him something of a hybrid, part Derbyite, part Groupist. According to *Shakespeare's Magic Circle,* the plays were products of "the combined wisdom of a group of outstandingly intelligent aristocrats, who met frequently, who had ample time on their hands, whose greatest relaxation in life was pursuit of the Muses, who themselves provided an adequate audience and the severest critics, led by one master mind." These "outstandingly intelligent aristocrats" formed the "magic circle" in which the plays were born. With diplomatic tact, Evans acknowledges the importance of the other members (most of them active candidates for the laurel themselves), but insists upon the leading role of "master mind" Derby. Among those whose talents Derby used were the Earls of Oxford and Rutland, Sir Francis Bacon, Sir Walter Raleigh, and the Ladies Pembroke and Rutland. In connection with the two last Evans finds it difficult to reject the idea of "some feminine influence," on the grounds that "a mere man" could not have written the line (misquoted), "All the yarn that Penelope spun in Ulysses' absence did but fill Ithaca with moths." An example of the group's democratic method of composition is *Hamlet,* probably first written by Oxford and then revised by Oxford and "master mind" Derby, with Rutland contributing some touches of local color. Throughout *Shakespeare's Magic Circle,* in fact, Evans, while remaining essentially true to Derby, shows a pleasing desire to let other Elizabethan aristocrats share in the glory of the plays.

The second member of the distinguished triumvirate with which this chapter is concerned was Roger Manners, fifth Earl of Rutland. Rutland's qualifications consist of the bluest blood and familiarity with the Court. According to the great biographer of his era, he was "an eminent traveller and good soldier" whose death in 1612 at the age of thirty-six has been explained in the *Dictionary of National Biography* on the grounds that "his constitution seems to have been worn out prematurely," a peaceful end in view of the Earl's penchant for duelling. Rutland's claims were rather cautiously set forth in 1906 by the mysterious Peter Alvor, who argued in a pamphlet entitled *Das Neue Shakespeare-Evangelium* that Rutland was the author of the Shakespearean comedies. (The histories and tragedies he reserved for Henry Wriothesley, Earl of Southampton, thereby differing from Walter Thomson, who in years to come was to see the Earl's hand in the comedies.) Alvor's arrangement irked the well-known German historian and man of letters, Karl Bleibtreu, who criticized Alvor in *Der Wahre Shakespeare* (1907), an unusual work consisting of a polemical introduction and a five-act drama based upon the author's Rutland theories. Before the year was out Alvor had replied with an enlarged edition of *Das Neue Shakespeare-Evangelium,* and Bleibtreu had further developed his case for Rutland as sole author in *Die Lösung der Shakespeare-Frage.* Alvor soon admitted defeat, switching to another candidate in 1911; Bleibtreu, on the other hand, flushed with victory, went on to publish another Rutland volume, *Shakespeares Geheimnis,* in 1923. His emphasis upon "Shakespeares Persönlichkeit" and his concern with what lay "Unter Shakespeares Maske" made it clear that Rutland's supporters were not above making use of Baconian techniques.

Bleibtreu's theories were soon embraced by the American, Lewis F. Bostelmann, who published, apparently some time around 1909, a four-act play variously entitled *Rutland, the*

Real Author of the Shakespearean Plays and *Roger of Rutland*. In 1911 Bostelmann brought forth, through the kindness of the "Rutland Publishing Company" of New York, a fuller explication of the mystery, bearing the well-rounded title:

Rutland, A Chronologically Arranged Outline of the Life of Roger Manners, Fifth Earl of Rutland, Author of the Works Issued in Folio in 1623 under the Nom de Plume "Shake-speare," Profusely Illustrated, Also a Drama Showing the Modus Operandi of the Engagement of William Shaxper of Stratford-on-Avon (second edition) as Dummy and Strawman for the Earl-Author, Amended and Greatly Augmented, and the Birth of the Folio, Showing How the Great Folio of 1623 Came Into Existence.

Ironically, neither Bleibtreu nor Bostelmann has been given the credit he deserves, and it has become customary to speak of a Belgian, M. Célestin Demblon, as the originator of the Rutland theory. Demblon, who combined a career in Belgian politics with the study of French literature, had embraced the Rutland theory as early as 1909, but it was not until 1912 that his first volume, *Lord Rutland est Shakespeare,* appeared. This was followed by *L'Auteur d'Hamlet et son Monde* in 1914. Both books attempt to prove that Rutland was the author by tracing the events of his life and then arguing that the Shakespearean plays merely echo Rutland's biography. The method forced Demblon to admit that in the early plays Rutland had depended heavily upon the works of other writers, notably Peele, Kyd, Marlowe, Greene, and Nashe. One of the Belgian's more interesting claims (based in part upon earlier researches of the Dane, Jon Stefansson) was that Rutland on a journey to Elsinore had seen an immense silken tapestry bearing portraits of the kings of Denmark. The remains of this tapestry, which Rutland had in mind when he caused Hamlet to stab Polonius through the arras, are still to be seen in a Copenhagen museum, according to Demblon.

Rutland's Demblon, lacking the energy and persistence of Derby's Lefranc, never succeeded in attracting a large following for his man. Although Karl Schneider's *Neues Zeugnis für Rutland-Shakespeare* appeared in 1932, the next important study of Rutland's claims did not come off the presses until 1940. Oddly enough, the author was a Russian, Pierre S. Porohovshikov, M.A. of Moscow University, Laureate of the Pushkin Award of the Russian Imperial Academy of Science (and Professor of History at Ogelthorpe University), and his book, *Shakespeare Unmasked,* owed more to Célestin Demblon than Professor Porohovshikov seemed willing to admit. With a generosity not unlike that of Derby's supporter, Evans, Porohovshikov made certain concessions to rival candidates, allowing Francis Bacon, for example, *Venus and Adonis* and *The Rape of Lucrece,* as well as *Love's Labour's Lost.* But in Porohovshikov's case they were made grudgingly. Forced to concede that the Folio was full of ciphers of "marvelous ingenuity and variety" which "no man but Bacon himself would have devised," Porohovshikov denied that their presence meant Bacon himself had written the plays. Granted that the philosopher was the editor of the Folio and the author of its ciphers, with the result that the "First Folio says *Bacon* in one language and *Rutland* in another," one should nevertheless avoid hasty inferences.

The dramas present the record not of Bacon's, but of Rutland's life. This brings us to a cruel enigma. Bacon's ciphered messages offer not the slightest hint of joint authorship. He claimed all the thirty-six plays of the Folio as his own. The inevitable conclusion is that he betrayed a dead friend as he had before betrayed, face to face, a man [Essex] who had been not his friend only, but his patron and benefactor.

Porohovshikov effectively destroyed at least one traditional counterargument of the Stratfordians. Admitting that someone was bound to ask how the monumental and long enduring secret of the bargain between Rutland the poet and "Shakspere the actor" could have been kept so well, he pointed out that history was full of safely guarded secrets. Who, he asked, was the Man in the Iron Mask? Who was Jack the Ripper? There can be no doubt, he concluded, that "in plain logic, the identity of the poet Shakespeare and Roger Manners appears to us as a moral certainty which, men of science tell us, is equivalent to mathematical certainty."

In a similarly confident manner, Porohovshikov faced up to another question, frequently ducked by supporters of the rival candidates: is there any evidence outside the disputed works themselves to show that the claimant possessed poetic talent? While Porohovshikov felt that "the real question is not whether Rutland had the titanic abilities requisite for writing the plays, but whether the circumstances of his life and his personal occupations are reconcilable with the surmise that he was their author," this professor of history did try to show, on the basis of evidence other than inferences from the plays, that Rutland was a literary man. Claiming an anonymous song printed in a *Booke of Ayres* (1599) for Rutland, he printed the first stanza of this sacred national heirloom, as he labeled it, as proof of his candidate's poetic genius.

> Farewell deare life since thou must needs be gone,
> myne eyes do see my life is almost done,
> nay, I will neu die, so long as I can spie
>> ther be many mo' though that she do go,
>> therebe many mo', I feare not
>> why then let her go, I care not.

The Rutland theory has not been popular in recent years. In 1947 Claud W. Sykes, recovering from Porohovshikov's demonstration, published *Alias William Shakespeare,* in which he claimed that "the methods of Sherlock Holmes identify Roger Manners, fifth Earl of Rutland as the man who shook the spear," and in 1955 *Shakespeare Unmasked* was reissued by a London firm. But at the moment the Rutland advocates seem to be playing what is at best a waiting game, hoping perhaps that the time will come when the process of natural selection will have made their task somewhat easier.

Both of the dashing courtiers previously discussed played parts in weakening the domination of the Baconian sect, and if none was capable by himself of posing a serious threat to the vogue for the Elizabethan philosopher, together they demonstrated beyond argument that Bacon's position, if impregnable from without, was vulnerable from within. The time was ripe for a new claimant to appear, one who could catch the imagination as Bacon had, but who would be free of some of the philosopher's manifold imperfections. This meant, specifically, someone of sufficient distinction to raise him above the crowd of ordinary courtiers; someone with a bit of a literary reputation, but lacking a large body of acknowledged works with which, embarrassingly, the Shakespearean plays would have to be compared; someone with, perhaps, a touch of mystery to his life, but without the public crimes of which Bacon had been adjudged guilty. Such a man was the Earl of Derby's father-in-law, Edward de Vere, seventeenth Earl of Oxford, a candidate whose support has been, excepting only that afforded Francis Bacon, without parallel in the history of the controversy.

Oxford, an Elizabethan nobleman known to have engaged in minor literary activity, appears to have been rather closely connected with the theater for a time. Although his supporters argue that he has not been treated kindly in the pages of history, it has been maintained at various times that he was quarrelsome as a youth to the point of fatally running a minor scullion through with a sword, a spendthrift who had no sense of honesty in handling his debts, and a philanderer specializing in the Queen's Maids-of-

Honour. However, with the exception of these rather conventional court activities, his life was not noticeably wicked.
The biographer John Aubrey relates that he was guilty of
an unfortunate flatulence in the presence of the Queen, a
bit of self-indulgence that is supposed to have been responsible for his long and mysterious continental sojourn. Oxford's blood lines, needless to say, were faultless.

The Earl's claims were worked out in detail by a Gates-
head School Master, J. Thomas Looney (not to be confused
with the Baconian, George M. Battey), "whilst the Great
European War was in progress." Looney, who, according to
an admirer, possessed "an intellectual range and a literary
and philosophical culture far beyond the requirements of
his professional avocation," had delivered a sealed letter
containing the results of his investigations to the librarian
of the British Museum as early as 1918, but did not publish
his discoveries until 1920, when *"Shakespeare" Identified
in Edward de Vere the Seventeenth Earl of Oxford* appeared. The issuance of this volume, described by a recent
Looney follower as an "epoch making work, which turned
the Maginot Line of Stratfordian orthodoxy," marked one
of the great moments in the Shakespeare controversy. The
Looney method, according to its originator, was "not an
accidental discovery, but one resulting from a systematic
search" for the real writer, a search pursued with some reluctance, apparently, for Looney seemed genuinely sorry
that he had been unable to avoid "hurting susceptibilities"
in the course of his work. The pattern, though, was a familiar one; after rather impatiently devoting some pages to
destroying the "tremendous mass of Stratfordian incongru-
ities and impossibilities"—impatiently because "outside the
ranks of those who have deeply committed themselves in
print it is indeed difficult nowadays to find any one in the
enjoyment of a full and assured faith"—Looney proceeded
to note the qualities of mind, temperament, and experience

revealed in the plays. He discovered nine "general features" possessed by the real author, who was:

1. A matured man of recognized genius.
2. Apparently eccentric and mysterious.
3. Of intense sensibility—a man apart.
4. Unconventional.
5. Not adequately appreciated.
6. Of pronounced and known literary tastes.
7. An enthusiast in the world of drama.
8. A lyric poet of recognized talent.
9. Of superior education—classical—the habitual associate of educated people.

A tenth "feature" was implied, though not listed: that "he" was not a self-made, self-educated man. In addition, the true poet revealed nine "special characteristics." He was:

1. A man with Feudal connections.
2. A member of the higher aristocracy.
3. Connected with Lancastrian supporters.
4. An enthusiast for Italy.
5. A follower of sport (including falconry).
6. A lover of music.
7. Loose and improvident in money matters.
8. Doubtful and somewhat conflicting in his attitude to woman.
9. Of probable Catholic leanings, but touched with scepticism.

Even Sir Sidney Lee was unable to cut Shakespeare of Stratford to this template. Not surprisingly, though, Looney found the pattern and Edward de Vere identical.

Looney admitted, in fact, to only one obstacle; Oxford's unfortunate demise in 1604, a death troublesomely early if one accepts the standard chronology for the plays. But, as Looney pointed out, "with the Earl of Oxford substituted for William Shakspere much of the guesswork relating to the time when the plays were *written* ceases to have any value." Only one play was able to stand up against this fiat —*The Tempest,* whose topical allusions seem to make it necessarily later than 1604. Looney, however, was "prepared to maintain" that " 'The Tempest' is no play of 'Shakespeare's.' " And he had some cogent arguments for his belief. If we accept the traditional view that it is a dramatic masterpiece, he argued, we must admit that chronologically speaking "it looks like a play that had wandered away and fallen into bad company," that is, into the company of such nondescript stuff as *Pericles* and *Henry VIII*. The comedy's "natural associate" would appear to be *A Midsummer Night's Dream,* suggesting strongly the probability of an earlier date. But, contended Looney, to argue this would be sheer sophistry, based on an uncritical acceptance of traditional evaluations of the play, and he was "indisposed to take refuge behind" such "findings." So he proceeded to demonstrate on various grounds that "this much belauded comedy" is actually second-rate and could not possibly be from the hand of the true author. Directing his onslaught against Prospero's " 'We are such stuff as dreams are made on, and our little life is rounded with a sleep,' " he concluded that the "sentence is in flat contradiction to the mind of Shakespeare," and that, furthermore, the whole passage is one of "metaphysical vagueness," filled with "the most dreary negativism that was ever put into high-sounding words." There being no question that "Shakespeare's soul was much too large for mere negation," the comedy could not possibly be from his hand. In this unilateral manner the last obstacle to the Oxford theory was safely removed.

Looney punctuated his discoveries the following year when he published a volume of Edward de Vere's poems, doubling the accepted number of Oxford's lyrics by annexing freely from other Elizabethans. John Lyly, for example, was relieved of the songs in his plays, on the grounds that he had "shown himself, in some of his work, to have been noticeably deficient in lyrical capacity," the songs being then given to Oxford as his "contribution" to Lyly's plays.

By claiming the signature "Ignoto" for the noble lord, Looney was able to coöpt poems attributed to Raleigh, Fulke Greville, and Richard Barnfield.

The Looney theory found ready acceptance from Colonel B. R. Ward, a Companion of St. Michael and St. George, who in 1922 formed the Shakespeare Fellowship with himself as *"Hon. Sec. and Treasurer."* Although Ward was an admitted Oxford man, the announced purpose of the Fellowship was "to unite in one brotherhood all lovers of Shakespeare who are dissatisfied with the prevailing Stratfordian orthodoxy, and desire to see the principles of scientific historical criticism applied to the problem of Shakespearean authorship." To maintain the proper balance, the vice-presidents included Mr. Looney, M. Lefranc, and Mr. William T. Smedley, a prominent Baconian, with the president, quite fittingly, being Sir George Greenwood. In later years, unfortunately, the Fellowship's fine catholicity was somewhat narrowed when first Lieutenant Colonel Montague W. Douglas, a Companion of the Order of the Star of India and of the Order of the Indian Empire, and then Admiral Hubert Henry Holland, a Companion of the Bath, succeeded to the presidency. Both were vigorous supporters of the Earl of Oxford.

The Fellowship had barely been organized when its founder, Colonel Ward, and its future president, the then Captain Holland, followed Looney into print. Neither Ward's *The Mystery of "Mr. W. H."* nor Holland's *Shakespeare Through Oxford Glasses* was accorded the reception given *"Shakespeare" Identified* three years earlier, and it became apparent that until more was known about Oxford himself, the Oxfordians, as they called themselves, could make little progress. What was needed was a detailed biography of the seventeenth Earl, one that would both clear his name of history's slanders and provide the necessary biographical material to explicate the Shakespearean plays and poems. Such a study, written by Colonel Ward's son, Captain Bernard Mordaunt Ward, appeared in 1928. Entitled *The Seventeenth Earl of Oxford, 1550–1604,* Ward's biography was praised by both the orthodox and the unorthodox camps for its wealth of historical detail. Unfortunately, from the former's point of view, Captain Ward seemed to have heretical opinions concerning Shakespeare that vitiated many of his conclusions about Oxford, and it is true that, without actually saying so, he gave the impression that the Shakespearean plays might have been written by an Oxford-Derby collaboration. Later, in letters to the London *Times* defending his biography, he made it clear that, at least in this matter, he was more comfortable in the company of heresy than of orthodoxy.

Just as, over seventy years before, Spedding's work on Bacon had given the candidacy of the Elizabethan philosopher a big boost, so now the appearance of Ward's biography with its recognizably anti-Shakespearean tone provided the spark necessary to move the seventeenth Earl's campaign into high gear. Among the first to exploit Ward's material was Percy Allen, son of a London lawyer who had renounced the world and become an "enthusiastic" member of the Plymouth Brethren, an evangelical Christian sect. Allen was a man of varied activities—drama critic for the *Christian Science Monitor,* author of travel books and one-act plays, compiler of a biography of his grandmother, the actress Fanny Stirling. In addition, he was interested in occult phenomena. Once possessed by the Oxford theory, he became a most voluble advocate, publishing his opinions with impressive regularity, and advertising himself as willing to lecture anywhere, any time. Like his contemporary, the Baconian Arensberg, Allen had engaged in a period of apprenticeship before coming to grips with this greatest of problems. In 1928 he had published a small volume designed to "shew that Jonson plagiarized systematically from

Shakespeare; and commented, in doing so, upon his texts";
in the next year he had brought out another book, this
one demonstrating that "Jonson's friend, Chapman, did
after his fashion, precisely the same thing." In the latter
study, emphasizing the topical nature of Shakespeare's
work, he argued that the Earl of Oxford was actually disguised in Hamlet. The stage, one might say, was set. In 1930
Allen came to the front with *The Case for Edward de Vere,
17th Earl of Oxford, As "Shakespeare"* (thoughtfully com-
posing a forty-two-page outline of his main arguments for
separate publication at the same time). The following year
saw *The Oxford-Shakespeare Case Corroborated,* and further volumes on the subject appeared during each of the
next three years. One of the orthodox writers with whom he
tilted was John Drinkwater, to whose criticism he replied at
length in 1933.

Among Percy Allen's more lasting contributions were his
discovery that the word "ipse" (*As You Like It*) spells
"Vere" in three simple ciphers, and his work on the dating
of *Hamlet.* Typical of the latter is his discussion of the
following lines:

> HAM. How long hast thou been a grave-maker?
> FIRST CLOWN. Of all the days i' th' year, I came to't the day that
>   our last King Hamlet o'ercame Fortinbras.
> HAM. How long is that since?
> FIRST CLO. Cannot you tell that? Every fool can tell that: it
>   was that very day that young Hamlet was born; he that is
>   mad, and sent into England.
> HAM. Ay, marry, why was he sent into England? . . . upon
>   what ground?
> FIRST CLO. Why, here in Denmark. I have been sexton here, man
>   and boy, thirty years.

Now these are very significant words, because if, as Capt. Holland surmises, we may for Denmark and Norway, read England and Scotland . . . the gravedigger's words mean, that he has

been practising his vocation since 1550, the year in which, during the reign of "our last King," Edward VI, peace was declared between the two countries, on April 1st; and as the clown further tells us, that he has been "sexton here, man and boy, thirty years," the date at which he is speaking is 1580, *when Oxford-Hamlet, born on April 12, 1550, was thirty* years old. The year 1580, therefore, may be taken as a key-date for the play; though other allusions tend to bring the year forward, a little, into the fifteen-'eighties; since the clown's reference to the skull of Yorick, the King's jester, as having "lain in the earth three-and-twenty years," points, almost certainly, to Will Somers, jester to King Henry VIII, who died in 1560, thus giving us not 1580, but 1583, as the year in which the clown is speaking.

Certain orthodox scholars have objected that Allen's "scientific historical criticism" is more in the tradition of Duns Scotus than of E. K. Chambers.

In later years Percy Allen's researches took a startling turn. Through the offices of a well known London medium, Mrs. Hester Dowden (daughter of the famous—and orthodox—Shakespearean, Edward Dowden), Allen was able to get in touch with his deceased brother Ernest, who in his turn managed introductions to Bacon, Oxford, and Shakespeare. Allen describes their conversations in *Talks With Elizabethans Revealing the Mystery of "William Shakespeare"* (1947).

Through the agency of a gifted medium, of wide experience and of unimpeachable integrity, I *have,* for many months past, been talking with the three above-named Elizabethans, from whom, sometimes by simple questioning, and sometimes upon their own initiative, I *have* obtained a series of answers and explanations, which—so far as I know—have provided, in some detail and for the first time, a *final* solution of the *Shakespeare* mystery, including the story of the harmless plot by means of which the name of the principal author, and of his collaborators, had hitherto been concealed. This work was accomplished through the willing cooperation of my medium's control, *Jo-*

hannes, without whose assistance nothing satisfactory could have been done.

The principal author was, not surprisingly, Oxford, aided by Shakespeare who specialized in plot construction (including the discovery of useful old plots), the creation of villains (Iago), comedy characters (Falstaff) and comedy scenes. Bacon supplied ideas, and other writers, among them Buckhurst, Paget, Raleigh, Beaumont, and Fletcher, occasionally lent a helping hand. But the poet of the group and the true creative spirit was Edward de Vere.

All this information was taken down by Mrs. Dowden in "automatic script": "the messages come, and are set down by her hand, which becomes the pen and instrument of her communicators." Mrs. Dowden had earlier performed the same service for Alfred Dodd, at which time Francis Bacon had revealed that he alone was responsible for the plays and poems. When questioned by Allen on November 7, 1944, about his seemingly contradictory assertions, Bacon replied:

F.B. My friend, I *can* help you. I was acting through a Deputy in the case of Dodd—a Deputy who has never been personally in touch with me, and who questions nothing; for he is firmly convinced that I wrote the plays and sonnets, and took no trouble to have a direct message from me.

P.A. Thank you. . . .

F.B. I shall be glad to refute Dodd.

At this point it seems somewhat anticlimactic to note that the conversations revealed that the manuscripts of the plays are in Shakespeare's tomb; or that the Earl of Oxford graciously composed three brand new sonnets for his friend, Mr. Allen.

Of almost equal stature in Oxford circles was the American, Mrs. Eva Turner Clark. Mrs. Clark, who had entered the controversy as early as 1926 with *Axiophilus; or, Oxford alias Shakespeare,* made her major contribution with *Hidden Allusions in Shakespeare's Plays* (1931: published in England as *Shakespeare's Plays in the Order of Their Writing*). One of the more important Oxford publications, it deserves a moment's scrutiny. Mrs. Clark's purpose was to establish a chronology that would fit Oxford's life and at the same time not necessitate damaging the critical repute of such plays as *The Tempest.* She accompanied this feat with astonishing ease, arriving at a sequence that began with *The Famous Victories of King Henry V* in 1574 and concluded with *Lear* in 1590, a play written "in bitterness of heart as a protest against the ingratitude shown him by the dissolution of his theatrical company." It might be objected that to try to explain the sublime agony of *Lear* on the grounds of the author's theatrical disappointments reveals a somewhat novel idea of artistic inspiration (and strikes at the heart of unorthodoxy's argument concerning literary cause and effect), but Mrs. Clark was blissfully unaware of these perils. However, Mrs. Clark's chronological reasoning needs quotation rather than comment:

Because of the belief that the Earl of Oxford was the writer of the plays attributed to William Shakespeare of Stratford, I came to the conclusion that they were written earlier than is generally supposed. It seemed probable that there should be some evidence of their early production on the stage in the records of the Court Revels. . . .

It was, then, to the titles of plays given at Court by the Lord Chamberlain's Company and by the Paul's Boys, from 1576 on, that I gave my attention. None of the titles in the records of the Court Revels are the same as titles belonging to any of the Shakespearean plays (or they would have been noted long ago), but, in a study such as I was making, several titles were suggestive. When I found a title which seemed to point to a certain Shakespearean play, I went carefully through the play, and then read the history of the period just previous to the date on which the title was recorded. If the events of the time were found alluded to in the play, the play of which the title had already caught my attention as suggestive of one of the Shakespearean plays, I felt justified in considering that my theory was in the course of being proved. After ten plays in succession were found to parallel in this fashion, I felt that the matter was no longer a theory but a demonstrated fact.

Among the suggestive titles, several of which revealed obvious clerical blunders, were:

> *The historie of the Solitarie Knight = Timon of Athens.*
> *The historye of Titus and Gisippus* (mistranscribed) *= Titus Andronicus.*
> *An history of the creweltie of A Stepmother = Cymbeline.*
> *A Morrall of the marryage of Mynde and Measure = The Taming of the Shrew.*
> *The historie of the Rape of the second Helene = All's Well that Ends Well.*
> *The history of Serpedon* (mistranscribed for "Cleopatra") *= Antony and Cleopatra.*

The historie of the Solitarie Knight is "suggestive" of Shakespeare's play, for example, because the latter "depicts Timon as being just as *solitary* in the midst of his grandeur as he later became in his cave in the woods." When, in addition, one realizes that during the decade of the seventies Oxford was deeply in debt, having reached a "crisis in his affairs, economically and socially," the conclusion is inescapable that we have here an example of "the events of the time" being "alluded to in the play." The truth of the matter, Mrs. Clark reveals amidst a cluster of images, is that *Timon of Athens* (original title, *Solitarie Knight*) was written by Oxford "from the bitterness of his soul because he had himself experienced the fawning and sugar-sweetness of fair-weather friends whilst he had money and spent it freely: then when his money gave out and he was temporarily out of favour with the Queen, he saw these friends drop away as if he had done something criminal."

Eva Turner Clark labored on for some years, examining *The Satirical Comedy, "Love's Labour's Lost"* from the Oxford point of view in 1933, and demonstrating Lord Oxford's "equipment for the part played by the greatest dramatist ever known" in *The Man Who Was Shakespeare* in 1937. In the meantime, other adherents of the seventeenth Earl were busy, with the result that during the nineteen-thirties the Oxford-Shakespeare controversy let almost as much ink as the Bacon-Shakespeare quarrel. Among the people publishing one or more books in support of Edward de Vere, were, in addition to those already mentioned, Gerald H. Rendall, Montague W. Douglas, George Frisbee, Gerald Phillips, Hubert Henry Holland, and Louis P. Bénézet, Doctor of Pedagogy. By far the most distinguished controversialist among them was Canon Rendall, variously Gladstone Professor of Greek and Principal at University College, Liverpool, Vice-Chancellor at Victoria University, Manchester, and Head of the famous Charterhouse School. A man of wide-ranging interests, as the titles of his published researches show, the Canon's major efforts included: *Shakespeare Sonnets and Edward De Vere* (1930), *Shake-speare: Handwriting and Spelling* (1931), *Personal Clues in Shakespeare Poems & Sonnets* (1934), and *Ben Jonson and the First Folio Edition of Shakespeare's Plays* (1939). One of his more important contributions was to refute the orthodox claim that Ben Jonson meant Shakespeare when he wrote Shakespeare in his Folio verses. Pointing out that Jonson "had frequent opportunities of personal touch with the Earl of Oxford, prior to his death in 1604" (it is hard to refrain from calling attention to the scholarly caution evinced by the Canon in the modifying phrase), Rendall abandoned the Baconian argument that Jonson was a liar and no gentleman and contended that he was a central and trusted figure in the great Folio Hoax. Ben Jonson did not, maintained the Canon, pass "over to the enemy," but remained loyal to the Oxford deception, "the skilled and most effective agent in the preservation of anonymity."

However, the Canon is best remembered for his investigation of the sonnets, and here he was not immune to the lure of the cipher, a tendency that Looney would certainly have deplored. Deservedly well known is his reading of the seventy-sixth:

> Why write I still all one, E. VER the same,
> And keep invention in a noted weed,
> That E. VERY word doth almost tell my name,
> Showing their birth and where they did proceed?

Were it not that Walter Arensberg had maintained with equal vigor that the same sonnet revealed Bacon as the true author, orthodox confidence might well have been shattered by this demonstration.

But perhaps the definitive work in the field of the cipher (Oxford variety) is that of George Frisbee. In *Edward De Vere: A Great Elizabethan* (1931), Frisbee's purpose was to "show that Edward Devere, 17th Earl of Oxford, was important in Elizabethan literary circles," so important, in fact, that his name popped up (albeit in disguise) wherever one happened to look. The demonstration was effected through Mr. Frisbee's inspired discovery that the six letters of Edward de Vere's name could be found in countless examples of Elizabethan writing. Frisbee's instructions and a brief demonstration of his method of deciphering will make clear the stunning simplicity of his book. First, the instructions:

NOTE: The *black* letters are to be read from the top to bottom; the *italic* letters from bottom to top; and the *black italic* letters are to be read in both directions in every example of cyphers throughout the book.

And now the demonstration. Let us look at one of the more unlikely places in which to find the Earl of Oxford's name buried, and see what Frisbee made of it. Our text is *The Famous Tragedy of the Rich Iew of Malta,* written by "Christopher Marlo" and published in 1633, twenty-nine years after Oxford's death. The Governor's speech concludes the play; it is given below with Frisbee's typographical emendations and comments.

> *Gov.:* Content thee, Calymath, here thou must stay,
> \> And live in Malta prison*e*r; f*or* come call th*e* wor**ld**
>   To **r**escue thee, so will we gua*r*d *vs* no**w**
>   As sooner shall they **d**rinke the Oc*e*an *d*ry,   <
>   Then conquer Malta, or en*d*ang**er** vs.
>   So ma*r*ch *aw*ay, and let *d*ue praise be gi*v*en   <
> \> Neither to Fat*e* nor Fortune, but to Heaven.

FINIS

Begin on "e" in "prisoner," read L. to R., spell "Edward Devere," end on "e" in "fate."

Begin on "e" in "fate," read L. to R., spell "Edward Devere," end on "e" in "prisoner."

"us," ll. 3 and 5, spell "vs."

According to Frisbee, one can scarcely find a piece of Elizabethan writing in which the author has not hidden references to Oxford's great secret in this manner.

That factor scholars like to call the exigency of space forces us to move on, ignoring the work of many other fine writers of the nineteen-thirties. The move is made with regret, however, for it would be valuable to consider more fully such theories as Admiral Holland's that Hamlet's "The time is out of joint" refers to the Continental change from the Julian to the Gregorian calendar; or Dr. Bénézet's that the sonnets were written *to* Shakespeare—Oxford's illegitimate son and an actor in his father's company. (It is

Begin on " e " in " pasture," read L. to R., spell
" E. Devere," end on " e " in " shepheard."

> I **never** drank of Aganippes well,
    No*r* **ev**e*r* di*d* in sha*d*e **of** Temp*e* *s*it :   <
> And Mu**s**es scorn with *v*ulgar brains to dw*e*ll,
    Poo**r** La**ym**an I, for sacred rites unfit.   <
> Som do I hear of Poets furie tell,
    But (God wot) wot n*o*t what the**y** mean by it :   <
> And this I sware by *b*lackest b*r*oo*k* of he*ll*,
    I am no pick-**p**urs of another's wit.   <
> How falls it th**e**n, that with so s***m***ooth an eas
    My thoughts I speak, and what I speak doth flow   <
> In ve*r*s, and that m*y* vers **b**est wits doth *p*lea*s*e ?
    Ghess wee the caus, wh*a*t is it thus ? fie no :   <
> A**r** **so** ? much less : how then ? sure thus it is :
    *M*y lips are sweet, inspired with Stt**e**lla's **k**iss.[1]

Begin on " e " in " never," read L. to R., spell " E.
Vere loves Mary Pembroke," end on " e " in " Sttella's."
    Begin on " m " in " my," read R. to L., spell " Mary
Pembroke loves Ed. Devere," end on " e " in " never."

> Good Brother Philip I hav**e** born you long
    I **w**as content you shoul**d** in favour creep   <
> While cr*a*ftily you seemed you**r** cut to keep,
    As though that fair soft hand **d**id you great **wrong** <
> I bar**e** (with envie) yet I bare your song,
    When in h**e**r n**e**ck you did Lo*v*e *d*itties peep ;   <
> Nay, more fool I, oft suffere*d* you to sleep
    In Lillie's n**e**ast, wh*e*re Love's solf lie's along.   <
> What, *d*oth high plac*e* ambitious thoughts **augment** ?
    Is sauriness rewar*d* of courtesie ?
> *C*annot such g*r*ace your silly self content,
    But you must needs *w*ith those lips billing bee ?
> And through those lips *d*rink Nectar from that tong :
    Leav that Sir Philip, lest off your n**e**ck bee wrung.[2]

[1] Sonnet 74, "Astrophel and Stella," *Countess of Pembroke's Arcadia*, p. 557.
[2] Sonnet 83, "Astrophel and Stella," *Countess of Pembroke's Arcadia*, p. 560.

Page showing typical solution of a cipher problem, from George Frisbee, *Edward De Vere* (Cecil Palmer, 1931).

worthy of note that two of Bénézet's colleagues in the Department of Philosophy at Dartmouth College used his hypothesis as an example of "The Logic of Truth," in a textbook entitled *Rational Belief* published in 1941. Neither philosopher is now at Dartmouth. Bénézet, on the other hand, is Emeritus Professor of Education.) But we must turn now to Charles Wisner Barrell and his epochal work.

While, with few exceptions, this survey has necessarily ignored periodical literature, one can hardly overlook Mr. Barrell's article in *Scientific American* for January, 1940, for it marks the entrance of modern scientific technology (as distinguished from scientific historical criticism) into the controversy. Entitled "Identifying 'Shakespeare' "—and pointedly left unendorsed by the editor—the article details the manner in which "Science in the Shape of Infra-red Photography and the X-ray Brings to Light at Last the Real Man Beneath the Surface of a Series of Paintings of the Bard." Although the "Series" turns out to be one painting, the so-called Ashbourne portrait ("Exigencies of space" prevent Mr. Barrell from telling us anything about his work on two other portraits), the scientific disclosures are certainly interesting, demonstrating, at least to the satisfaction of the tyro, that the canvas has at some time been painted over. According to Barrell, the likeness revealed underneath the present pigment is that of Oxford. It is at this point in Mr. Barrell's article that the orthodox gorge has been known to rise, for he continues, "as the penetrative eye of modern photographic science is focused more sharply upon this extraordinary picture-puzzle, more and more evidence accumulates to argue that we have at last found a visual key to the age-old mystery of 'William Shakespeare's' real personality." In other words, Oxford was Shakespeare.

One hesitates these days to break lances with a man of science, especially when he is a distinguished member of the "Shakespeare Fellowship (American Branch)" and author of *Elizabethan Mystery Man: A Digest of Evidence Connecting Edward De Vere, 17th Earl of Oxford, with the Literary Activities of "Mr. William Shakespeare."* Nevertheless, it would be something less than objective to fail to report that the Ashbourne portrait is (outside of Oxford circles) not held to be genuine, being considered by most authorities as another example of an earlier age's traffic in spurious Shakespeare portraits, an illicit trade of some proportions before the days of modern iconography. As a result, while orthodox Shakespeareans praise Mr. Barrell for the brilliant discovery of a long-lost Oxford painting, they insist with old-fashioned logic that the mere fact of some nineteenth-century hack's having painted the Lord over with a likeness of the actor proves no more than that their man had an even higher market value than a seventeenth earl.

Although the intense activity of the years between 1930 and 1940 has not been equaled, the Oxford theory has remained popular, especially in America, where de Vere has largely replaced Bacon as the leading contender. The present writer recalls seeing a play based upon the theory during the summer of either 1940 or 1941. It was produced at McCarter Theatre in Princeton and may have marked the first time that a drama inspired by the Shakespearean controversy had appeared in a professional production. (Mrs. Natalie Clark sponsored some amateur performances on her Dial stage.) The play was not very good and made little impression at the time, the writer then being unversed in the mysteries of literary history. In 1942 William Kittle's *Edward de Vere, 17th Earl of Oxford and Shakespeare* appeared, published after Kittle's death by the Monumental Printing Company of Baltimore, and, a few years later, the prankishly entitled *Edward de Vere, the Seventeenth Earl of Oxford, the Real Shakespeare, by William Kent and Another*. Important too in keeping the theory alive have been the newsletters of the Shakespeare Fellowship, by now thoroughly infiltrated with Oxford's supporters. It was not, however, until 1947 that the man who is currently Oxford's most voluble advocate put in his appearance with *The Renaissance Man of England,* a book that, in the light of what was to come, must be considered merely a piece of preliminary research. It was only when the author, an American lawyer named Charlton Ogburn, was joined by his wife Dorothy (something of a literary figure in her own name, she had written a little piece called *Ra–ta–plan—!* in 1930) that the fruits of his husbandry truly ripened. Their coeffort, *This Star of England: "William Shakespeare" Man of the Renaissance* (1952), is a volume of twelve hundred and ninety-seven pages (with illustrations), making it the most ambitious publishing venture in the annals of the controversy. Yet for all the book's vastness, the Ogburns' thesis is not unfamiliar. William Shaksper ("or Shagsper, or Shakspe, or Shaxper, as it was variously written") was an oaf, or to be more accurate, "an obscure young grain-dealer," who was "uneducated, unlettered, undistinguished, and virtually unknown." To identify this rustic with the "brilliant, highly cultivated, worldly, intuitive genius whose self-portrait emerges unmistakably from the series of nobly born Shakespearean heroes, imposes upon us not merely a misconception of the personality behind the dramas but a misconception of the origins of all artistic production." This identification we have been traditionally obliged to make by what the Ogburns describe as "the most amazing literary hoax of all time."

This Star of England is filled with an impressive amount of historical information concerning Oxford's known and reputed activities, activities which the Ogburns profess to see woven into the plays by means of an ingenious allegory. According to them, one has only to look with an open mind and "identity-clues" appear like locusts, each one revealing

Edward de Vere as the true author. One example will suffice: Rosalind's statement in *As You Like It* that "men are
April when they woo, December when they wed." This,
maintain the Ogburns, "recalls the fact that Oxford, born in
April, wooed when very young and was quite cool by the
time of his December wedding."

Mr. and Mrs. Ogburn reveal themselves as typical dissenters in other ways, too, surrendering, for one thing, to
the temptation to annex other writers' efforts for their own
candidate. Thus they cannot allow Kyd to keep *The Spanish Tragedy,* as "it would have been a miracle for the son
of a scrivener, educated in the Merchant Taylors school, to
have written so courtly a drama, showing special knowledge of nobles in battle, actors in Italy, and other matters
requiring unusual sophistication." (Perhaps what appears
from the distance to be a kind of unnecessary acquisitive-
ness on the part of many non-Shakespeareans is actually an
unavoidable syndrome of Dr. Titherley's "literary sincerity," a principle to which all sceptics must in the end
subscribe, for the number of true noblemen among the
Elizabethan playwrights was not large, and Elizabethan
dramatic literature is embarrassingly full of kings and
queens and courts and battles and so forth. In this connection it may not be out of place to recall a noted professor
of Greek who breathed a sigh of relief when informed that
Titherley's principle does not necessarily apply to classical
drama.)

The Ogburns argue also that the Earl of Southampton
was really the son of Oxford and Elizabeth, something
more than "simply a royal bastard," however, for "we cannot but suppose that his birth, or his parents' union, had in
some way been 'legitimatized,' or sanctioned by the
Church." Therefore the sonnets supposedly addressed to
the poet's friend, the "Fair Youth" as the Ogburns call
him (emphasizing the frequent appearance of this particu-

lar phrase) were actually written to a son by his father. Central to this thesis is the Ogburns' respect for the Elizabethan pun. Fair Youth, Vere Youth—Q.E.D.! Although B. M. Ward, Percy Allen, and numerous Baconians had in their time been aware that something was amiss in the Queen's household, the Ogburns stress that "it must, however, be stated that we had arrived at the conclusion that Southampton was the son of Oxford and the Queen almost a year before we heard that anyone else had entertained the suspicion."

It might be supposed that twelve hundred and ninety-seven pages (with illustrations) of such closely reasoned arguments as those demonstrated in the "Fair Youth" deduction would rather exhaust the possibilities of the Oxford theory, at least for awhile, but such has not been the case. Montague Douglas published a revision of *Lord Oxford and the Shakespeare Group* in the same year that *This Star of England* appeared, and since then, if the theory has not been promulgated with quite the frequency of the decade of the thirties, it has nevertheless been demonstrating a healthy persistence. In 1955 the Ogburns revised *The Renaissance Man of England,* and Hilda Amphlett, an Englishwoman, published *Who Was Shakespeare? A New Enquiry* (with an introduction by Christmas Humphreys), demonstrating her scholarly independence by ignoring completely the impressive amount of material to be found between the covers of *This Star of England.* (Miss Amphlett's failure even to mention the Ogburns is another unfortunate example of the chauvinism that has tended to mar the Oxford effort, which has never been marked by the air of international goodwill that characterized the activity on behalf of Bacon.) In 1956, the reader may recall, Oxford's supporters took the unusual step of inserting a paid advertisement in the orthodox *Shakespeare Newsletter* in order to remind the traditionalists of their blindness. Like the

Derby theory, the Oxford thesis appears to have sufficient momentum to carry it along for some years to come.

The Shakespearean sceptics discussed in this chapter choose to think of themselves as a different breed from the Baconians, for whose ciphers and secret societies they demonstrate frequent scorn. The reader may, however, have detected more similarities than differences. In their arguments for the negative case, that is, the case against Shakespeare, they reveal the same class-consciousness demonstrated by Bacon's supporters, the same impatience with the unromantic picture of the Stratford man that history has handed down to us. In arguing the positive case, most of them, not unlike the Baconians, have their dream of what a poet should be and are willing to make every effort to see this dream come true. Typically, this effort consists of amassing as much historical and semihistorical information about their own particular Elizabethan earls as they can, and then interpreting the Shakespearean works literally in relation to this information. Whether the assumption that dramatic action and dramatic characters must necessarily allude to real actions and to real people is a valid principle of "scientific historical criticism" I leave to the reader to decide.

Act V

MOST RARE VISION

A Midsummer Night's Dream, IV, i

The reader must not assume that the claims made for Bacon, Derby, Rutland, and Oxford have been opposed only by orthodox Shakespeareans. The truth is that the major aspirants have had to battle a bewildering array of would-be Shakespeares. The number and variety of these minor candidates (minor, at any rate, in the sense that their backers have never succeeded in gaining widespread popular support) is astonishing, and their colorful ranks certainly deserve at least a hurried glance. The brief survey that follows is just that—a far from exhaustive account of some of the more provocative theories, the candidates involved being in addition to those proposed by advocates of the various group theories.

We will pass over the sonnets, which have been fathered upon such heterogeneous Elizabethans as Anthony Bacon, Raleigh, Sidney, Southampton, Marlowe, Barnes, Warner, Donne, and Daniel, and turn directly to the plays. Here, the search for the author has not been limited to England, as candidates have included an Italian, a Frenchman named Jacques Pierre, and an Irishman, Patrick O'Toole of Ennis. The Irish theory, advanced by George Newcomen in 1897, was revived (without, however, identifying Shakespeare as O'Toole) by T. F. Healey in 1940. Healey's delightful Gaelic imagination must have caused the editors of the *American Mercury* some uncertain moments before they decided to print his arguments, particularly his contention that Hamlet is an Irishman whose character is largely based on an "Irish tradition that Hamlet's was a tailoring family." This is proved by the play's many references to clothing. Naturally, the ghost is also Irish, revealing his nationality in the lines which describe his having "for a certain term to walk the night." Healey's comment on the ghost's speech is worth citing.

Here we have speaking a real or an Irish ghost; indeed, Hamlet's father is the dead spit of an Irish ghost, being rational, forthright and purposeful. The English never had a rational ghost, and their spectres are unreal. Every Irish ghost has personality.

Similar to these extra-national theories was Harold Johnson's thesis that the plays were written by the Company of Jesus, set forth in *Did the Jesuits Write "Shakespeare"?* in 1916. Nor should Mr. Finch Barnard be overlooked, for, according to Charles J. Finger, around 1921 he "identified the poet as a collateral of his own, other ornaments of the same family, including (to go no higher) Charlemagne and St. Francis of Assisi." Closer to home are the theories involving women. In addition to Queen Elizabeth, Mary Queen of Scots has been proposed as the author, her champion, A. Ramsay, setting forth his views in 1913. Of a humbler nature, and therefore more surprising in view of the traditional objections to William Shakespeare, is the claim that Anne Hathaway (or Mrs. Shakespeare, as her supporters call her) wrote the plays. This theory was advanced by Conrad Seiler in 1936 and again by J. P. De Fonseka in 1938. The "Mrs. Shakespeare" theory was followed closely by the Anne Whateley theory, about which more will be said later. A rather modest claim was that of Louis C. Alexander in *The Autobiography of Shakespeare* (1911), who maintained that the poet was not "the reckless or besotted youth" who gained credit for the plays, but his cousin William, son of "Richard Shakspere of Warwicke" who had changed his name from Little. Thus Alexander, to his own satisfaction at least, got rid of the unsavory Stratford connections while retaining the magic name of Shakespeare.

As might be supposed, a number of candidates have come from the ranks of recognized Elizabethan writers. In addition to Marlowe, the names of Ben Jonson and Barnabe Barnes have been brought forward, the latter having been described as Shakespeare's "literary devil." More successful was the campaign on behalf of Robert Burton, initiated in 1885 by M. L. Hore and lasting as late as 1921, when there was still some discussion of the Burton-Shakespeare theory. But, not surprisingly, the largest number of minor candidates have been Renaissance noblemen or gentlemen whose superior breeding has been in welcome contrast to the Stratford man's red yeoman blood.

The first of these socially acceptable Elizabethans to be proposed was Sir Walter Raleigh, to whose candidacy we shall return in a few pages. He was followed by Sir Anthony Sherley, a relatively obscure gentleman who seems to have been something of a traveler and who was a protégé of the Earl of Essex. His claims were advanced in 1888 by the Reverend Scott Surtees, of Dimsdale-on-Tees, in a small book entitled *William Shakespere, of Stratford-on-Avon. His Epitaph Unearthed, and the Author of the Plays Run to Ground*. They were given further support by C. Shirley Harris in 1897. In 1905, in *Shake-speare: England's Ulysses,*

Latham Davis took the inevitable step, parting the protégé from the dramas, and presenting them to the patron, Robert Devereux, second Earl of Essex. The next year, it may be recalled, Peter Alvor, in the course of starting the Rutland movement, assigned the histories and tragedies to the pen of Henry Wriothesley, Earl of Southampton. Within a year J. E. Nicol had added the comedies, but Southampton's cause was to languish thereafter until the appearance of Walter Thomson in the thirties. In the meantime, Alvor, never one to stay with a loser, was back within a few years with a new candidate, Anthony Bacon, brother of Sir Francis. The ground had been prepared for the appearance of this theory as far back as 1897, when an anonymous article in *Baconiana* had asked if Anthony Bacon had not actually been the greatest minor Elizabethan poet, author of, among other things, the works of Ben Jonson and Montaigne. Thus Alvor's proposal in *Die Lösung des Shakespeare-Problems* (1911) that Anthony had written the Shakespearean plays was not as great a feat of the imagination as it might at first glance appear. Alvor's theory was still being supported twenty years later by W. H. Denning, who between 1925 and 1933 appeared in print regularly on Anthony Bacon's behalf. But by this time Alvor had switched to still another candidate, maintaining in *Eine Neue Shakespeare-Biographie* (1930) that it was Charles Blount who had been the real author. Blount, Earl of Devonshire and eighth Lord Mountjoy, was a notable warrior and pacifier of the Irish, as well as a Knight of the Garter. In his maturer years, we learn, he had been the lover and later husband of Sidney's "Stella." But in spite of these seemingly irresistible attractions, he failed to win the approval of the anti-Shakespearean intelligentsia.

While Alvor had been supporting and then deserting Anthony Bacon, another name had been suggested, that of Robert Cecil, first Earl of Salisbury. His advocate was John

M. Maxwell and the time was around 1916. In 1937 Alden Brooks began the researches that were to lead him to Sir Edward Dyer within a few years, and in 1953 Ira Sedgwick Proper spoke out on behalf of William Seymour, the "bastardized" son of the Earl of Hertford and Lady Catherine Grey. *Our Elusive Willy, A Slice of Concealed Elizabethan History* is an impressive book of well over six hundred pages, but it is not half so impressive as the thesis it presents. According to Proper, the infant William Seymour was handed over to Mary Shakespeare, whose own child had died at birth. Mary's major qualification for the task of rearing the noble lad appears to have been her lactiferous capacity; at any rate, the bargain was struck and the child given the "legal or baptismal name" of William Shakespeare. Arriving at manhood, Seymour-Shakespeare soon became the central figure in the literary and political life of the capital, functioning under many different aliases, including such names as Christopher Marlowe, John Southerne, John Dowland, John Smith, Thomas Morley, Thomas Campion, Richard Barnfield, Henry Constable, and Alfonso Ferrabosco. The various accomplishments, literary, musical, and otherwise which history has ascribed to these men were, of course, Seymour's, along with the Shakespearean plays and poems. Actually, if Proper's word is to be taken, very little artistic activity went on outside the Seymour family, for the Earl of Hertford's alias was Spenser, his half-brother, Lord Seymour's, was Lyly, while Barnabe Rich, Thomas Lodge, Robert Greene, Michael Drayton, John Marston, Francis Beaumont, and John Ford were all pen names of various other Seymours.

Thus the campaign for Shakespeare's crown has been varied as well as persistent, and any ranking of leading contenders is bound to be arbitrary and to create a certain amount of unhappiness on the part of the supporters of those overlooked. Of the selection of the half-dozen candidates now to be considered in greater detail, the only fense offered is that they all fulfill the first requirement having had their claims presented in at least one boo length publication, and that as a group they represent the nature and extent of the purlieus of dissent about as accurately as one could wish. The reader will note that the organization of material in this chapter is different from that used previously, the roughly chronological order of the earlier chapters having been modified here in accordance with principles that will be quite obvious as this account progresses.

Nevertheless, we will begin with what appears to have been the first candidate to challenge the eminence upon which Bacon sat exalted—Sir Walter Raleigh. Raleigh, it will be recalled, had figured prominently in Delia Bacon's group theory, a theory that seems to have appealed to Walt Whitman, who about this time (1857) was arguing that Sir Walter (along with Bacon) had had a hand in the plays. But it was an Australian, George S. Caldwell, who first made a strong case for Elizabeth's erratic favorite, in a pamphlet published at Melbourne in 1877 and entitled *Is Sir Walter Raleigh the Author of Shakespeare's Plays and Sonnets?* While Caldwell's arguments do not seem to have made much of an impression, the Raleigh theory was advanced again, around the middle of the eighteen nineties, by the silver-tongued Senator from Indiana, Albert J. Beveridge. Presented before a meeting of the Indianapolis Literary Club, the argument that Senator Beveridge brought forth in favor of Sir Walter is described by his biographer as a bit of youthful literary enthusiasm he gladly would have forgotten in later years; still, he appears to have been serious enough at the time, for he made more than one attempt to have his paper published, an immortality it never attained, by the way. Beveridge's opening remarks were conventional, merely effecting the traditional disposal of the Stratfordian. However, when he proceeded to eliminate that "cold diplomat" and "corrupt intriguer," Bacon, on the grounds that he "had no warm generous blood" and therefore "intrigue with a woman would have been impossible with this slow-pulsed, calculating politician," the Senator was making history. Coming from outside the orthodox camp, and at the full tide of the Baconian movement, such a spirited attack on the great philosopher was unusual indeed. Even more so was the central idea on which the Senator was to base his novel argument for Raleigh. Beveridge's point was simply taken; he felt that the plays "flame with animal passion," that "everywhere the spasm of propagation is in full ecstasy," and that one must find, therefore, an author possessing a certain elemental ardor among his other characteristics. When the Senator discovered that Sir Walter Raleigh, adventurer, courtier, and man of letters, was reputed to have been capable of seducing one of the Queen's maids at the age of forty, he knew that he had found his man.

The management of Raleigh's campaign was taken over in the next century by Henry Pemberton, Jr., of Philadelphia, whose articles on the subject began appearing in 1906. In 1914, the year after his death, Pemberton's definitive study of the candidate's claims, *Shakspere and Sir Walter Ralegh,* was published. Comfortably assuming, as had the Senator, that it would have been impossible for the Stratford actor to have written the plays, Pemberton proceeded to analyze the Shakespearean works for suggestions of Sir Walter's life and character. Needless to say, he found many. In two references to lameness in the sonnets (held by orthodoxy to be figurative), he found proof of Raleigh's authorship. There is no evidence that Shakespeare was lame, Pemberton pointed out, while it is a fact that Raleigh was wounded in 1596: *ergo!* Similarly, Hamlet's "O villain, villain, smiling damned villain!" must be interpreted in terms of the Raleigh theory, for it is a line which attacks a king "in language so violent that a parallel cannot be found in any Drama of our language." Only Raleigh's great hatred of James I, to whom the words obviously refer, could explain such rage.

One of Pemberton's more revealing accomplishments was the identification of Yorick's skull. It is central to the methodology of modern opponents of Stratford orthodoxy that no allusion in the canon be left unexplained, no reference, however trivial, be permitted to slip by without having had its historical basis pointed out. The idea that the writer might actually have imagined something is, of course, contrary to the very core of the logic of dissent. Thus no respectable practitioner could afford to leave a skull lying around, unidentified and unexplained. The particular one handled by Hamlet was, according to Pemberton, that of John Heywood, poet, playwright, and epigrammatist, the date of whose death falls within such broad limits that it might easily have occurred "three and twenty years" before the composition of *Hamlet*. Without going into Pemberton's reasons for choosing Heywood as the skull's former owner (Percy Allen was to identify it as Will Somers' before long), let me quote a few lines from his argument that the reference to Yorick must be taken as referring to a real person, for the concept of literary imagination lying behind them is basic to an understanding of the Shakespeare controversy.

Another point to be derived from the Grave-digger's remarks, is, that his references to Yorick are undoubtedly biographical in character. Such a very definite number as twenty-three would not have been selected unless the writer of the scene had in mind some actual person who had died at the time stated. Had he said "twenty years" it would have been different; for the word "twenty" is used throughout the plays as a comprehensive term of quantity, similar to the phrase "a thousand times" that Hamlet uses in describing his childish frolics with Yorick. But the Second Quarto (1604) gives the number in figures (thus: "23.") So, likewise, do the Third and Fourth Quartos. The Fifth Quarto and the Folio, give it in words, ("twenty-three" and "three and twenty," respectively). There can thus be no likelihood of a misprint or typographical error having occurred. A direct biographical reference, therefore, must be accepted as having been made in the Second Quarto (written in 1601–2), this Quarto being the first impression of the play, as we now have it. And the same is true of the remarks of Hamlet regarding Yorick, as will be shown presently.

Curiously enough, Raleigh, an established literary figure whose varied life and conflicting moods do suggest something of the infinite variety of the plays, has not been a popular candidate. His failure may be in part the result of historical accident, his early advocates appearing on the scene before Edwards had made desertion of Bacon profitable. To some extent it may also be related to his pedigree, as Raleigh is not equal from a genealogical point of view to other more vigorously supported candidates. That this is an important consideration the reader will recognize; in Raleigh's case not even the backing of a Philadelphian was able to overcome it.

A similar lack of titles may be responsible for the failure of the Dyer theory. Sir Edward Dyer, a minor courtier and a minor poet, was proposed as Shakespeare's substitute almost fifteen years ago by Alden Brooks, a minor American novelist and autobiographer who served in the French Army during what is sometimes known as the first unpleasantness. Astutely refusing to assume the negative case as proved, Brooks began his campaign in 1937 with *Will Shakspere, Factotum and Agent,* a volume devoted to showing that Shakespeare of Stratford was not the true author. At the same time he promised another volume dedicated to "the task of establishing the identity of the poet." This appeared as *Will Shakspere and the Dyer's hand* in 1943. It did not ignite a crusade.

Alden Brooks, not unexpectedly, maintained that Will was nothing more than a boorish, if witty, country boy who became a playbroker (and in his later years, a brothel keeper). Among other things, he acted as literary agent for Dyer, who modestly published his work over Shakespeare's name, apparently ignoring his agent's unsavory reputation. Brooks makes much of Shakespeare's bad habits, describing him as a "tavern frequenter" whose "swagger and pretense were immense; his morals, of a low standard." According to those "whose ill-will he aroused" (almost everyone in Elizabethan England, in Brooks' opinion) he was a "fool, knave, usurer, vulgar showman, illiterate bluffer, philanderer, pandar, and brothel keeper" who drove a hard bargain and pursued defaulters relentlessly. The manner in which Brooks creates this portrait is interesting, if not wholly new. Shakespeare being in his eyes a veritable Prince of Boors, he feels that any reference in Elizabethan literature that even hints at boorishness must perforce be a reference to "Will Shakspere." For example: Shakespeare was known as a town wit. According to Brooks, it follows that "he must then have been further at least a little vain by nature and something of a braggart, and when attacked, quick to give answer." In addition, he "drove hard bargains." Therefore, one must look for references to these traits in contemporary literature. Such traits were dramatized by Robert Greene in *Selimus* in the person of a character known as Bullithrumble.

In what individuality Bullithrumble possesses there seems to be a direct rap at Will himself. It is indeed as if Greene were saying, "Ah, you want a comic figure! Well, you shall have one."

First of all, mark the name: Bullithrumble. A "bulli" is a "bully"; Holland, in his translation of Plutarch, gives us a definition of "thrumble"—"gather, thrumble, and heap up together all sort of gain." Bullithrumble is thus a bully who heaps up gain.

Thus, it has been demonstrated that Bullithrumble is an allusion to Shakespeare because Bullithrumble is represented as being both a bully and a profit-seeker. This, in turn, proves that Shakespeare was a bully and a profit-seeker, because Bullithrumble is modeled directly upon him. The logic is not unlike that used by Percy Allen to date Oxford's *Hamlet*. It also makes inevitable Brooks' thesis that Falstaff is a caricature of "Will Shakspere," an argument at least as old as Ignatius Donnelly's *The Great Cryptogram*.

Another of Brooks' learned hypotheses is that John Webster, when praising the "right happy and copious industry of Mr. Shake-speare, Mr. Dekker, and Mr. Heywood" in the address "To the Reader" of *The White Devil*, deliberately spells Shakespeare's name with a hyphen to suggest Dyer's authorship. It is to be regretted that the value of this revelation is lessened by Brooks' carelessness in transcribing Webster's words. The lines are actually in italics (a hint that no Baconian would have overlooked) and more importantly, the three gentlemen named are given as *"M. Shake-ſpeare, M. Decker, & M. Heywood,"* a coincidence that the advocate of Jacques Pierre also overlooked, I believe.

In his arguments on Sir Edward Dyer's behalf, Brooks is characterized more by plenitude than by originality. After listing fifty-four qualifications that the Poet must be prepared to meet, he arbitrarily dismisses rival claimants with such pontifical statements as "'Ever' and 'every' are words too common to be taken, wherever used, as offering a pun on the name 'E. Vere.'" His own arguments are in striking contrast to such historical naïveté. Typical is his sophisticated handling of the sixth qualification, which states that "the Poet possessed a deceptive public manner." In the chapter called "Concordance with the Pattern," Brooks reveals that Dyer's "courtly urbanity was a deceptive public manner that constantly hid his private thought and opinions," thus causing him to fit qualification number six with unmatchable precision. In a similar fashion, Sir Edward is made to fit the fifty-three other specifications.

Brooks depends heavily upon the citation of parallel passages. He points out that Dyer, in a known poem, wrote, "He that his mirth has lost"; and then finds a significant echo in *Hamlet,* "I have of late . . . lost all my mirth." Significant, too, is the reappearance of Dyer's "And so an end, my tale is told" as the "Even so; my tale is told" of *Love's Labour's Lost;* and his phrase "shrieking shrill" as "Your shrill-shrieking daughters" in *Henry V.* Indeed, Brooks can conceive of only one possible objection to Dyer—he died before many of the plays had appeared. But with traditional aplomb, Brooks extricates himself from his dilemma by reasoning that everything in the canon supposedly written after Dyer's death in 1607 must actually represent early work. Irrefragable proof of the validity of this hypothesis is found in *The Tempest,* for "the fact that *The Tempest* occupies first place in the First Folio suggests that it was indeed one of the earliest of the Shakespearean plays." Brooks' handling of chronology is more breath-takingly simple than even the Looney solution discussed in the previous chapter.

More imaginative are the arguments of Signor Santi Paladino, born one restless night as he lay brooding upon a fortuneteller's prediction that he was to make to the world an "importante rivelazione." Paladino's "rivelazione" turned out to be "importante" indeed, for it was nothing less than the belief that Shakespeare was actually an Italian, Michel Agnolo Florio by name. Florio, a Protestant refugee who had found his way to England, was the father of the well-known John, compiler of proverbs, author of popular dialogues and an Italian-English dictionary, and famous translator of Montaigne. According to Paladino's thesis, Michel Agnolo Florio, a victim of Romish persecution, had been afraid to print the "lavori cosiddetti shakespeariani" in his own name, but when youthful John Florio made the acquaintance of youthful William Shakespeare the idea occurred of publishing the so-called Shakespearean works through the offices of the English actor, an arrangement that would enable the older Florio to realize a bit of a profit on his long-hidden plays. Drama after drama was "tradotte in buon inglese dal figlio," a son who did not hesitate to help himself to some of his father's lesser works in the process. The secret, known only to a few people, was successfully kept for centuries until the inspiration of Santi Paladino, for whom it was a matter of national pride to set the record straight.

Paladino's discovery, made one night in 1925, was published two years later in the Italian newspaper *L'Impero.* His arguments were presented more fully in 1929 in the "volumetto," *Shakespeare sarebbe il pseudonimo di un poeta italiano?* a work which drew more than a thousand responses, according to its author, most of which aligned their writers "solidali con me." With all this backing, the formation of an "Accademia Shakespeariana" was inevitable. The Academy was dedicated to the memory of Michel Agnolo Florio, and, according to the Italian correspondent of the London *Times,* to "the waging of polemics with the national and foreign Press." With what was perhaps a touch of insularity, the correspondent noted that "in this objective at least the academicians of Reggio Calabria appear likely to be successful." This satisfaction was to be denied them, however; four days after the *Times'* first notice, a dispatch was published reporting that the Academy was in difficulty with the local authorities. By 1930 the political powers had forced the members to cease their activities, confiscated Paladino's materials, and prohibited the sale of his book, which, he complains, had been going like hot cakes ("andato a ruba"). Thus a most provocative thesis appeared to be doomed by political meddling. In view of its far-reaching intercultural implications, it is good to be able to report that in 1955 Signor Paladino renewed his campaign with *Un italiano autore delle opere Shakespeariane,* claiming that "l'ipotesi di ieri è per diventare la certezza di domani."

Whether today's hypothesis becomes tomorrow's certainty remains to be seen. Signor Paladino has suggested the direction in which further proof is to be found, stressing particularly the necessity for further investigation of that old favorite of the Baconians and the supporters of Derby, the comedy *Pene d'amore perdute.* More significant than Paladino's own confidence, however, is the backing the Italian theory has had from, of all places, Germany. In 1927 Erik Reger came to the support of "Der Italiener Shakespeare," and in 1954 Friderico Georgi (Franz Saalbach) elaborated upon Paladino's theory in *William Shakespeare alias Mercutio Florio,* also making the not unpredictable claim that the author of *Hamlet* had also written "Dr. Faustus, der Spanischen Tragödie, der Fairy Queen, der Apology of Poetry und des Euphues, um nur einige Werke zu nennen."

The distance between the Florio theory and the one to which we turn now is great only in terms of geography and gender. This time the supposed author is an Englishwoman, a lady whose literary career makes that of the famed Countess of Pembroke seem amateurish by comparison. To comprehend the theory fully, however, it is necessary, by way of preface, to spend a moment on some puzzling facts of Shakespearean biography. The Bishop of Worcester's Register for November 27, 1582, has an entry for a marriage license "inter Willelmum Shaxper et Annam Whateley de Temple Grafton." The very next day it records a bond of surety for the marriage of "William Shagspere on thone partie, and Anne Hathwey of Stratford in the Dioces of Worcester maiden." Most orthodox scholars feel that the Register simply lists two of the necessary steps preparatory to the marriage of William Shakespeare of Stratford (the variations in orthography are typical of Elizabethan practice, they contend, pointing out that Shakespeare's will is signed with three different spellings of his name). The difficulty arises over the attempt to explain the Anne Whateley of the first entry, for there is general agreement that Anne Hathaway was his wife's true name. The most common explanation is that "Whateley" represents scribal carelessness and that "Temple Grafton" was where the marriage was to take place; but conservative scholars emphasize that this is merely a guess—a logical and cautious guess, perhaps, but incapable of proof, nevertheless. There is, at any rate, no evidence that Anne Whateley was ever anything but the product of a clerk's careless pen.

With the historical facts in mind, let us now turn to the deductions made from them by William Ross, Fellow of the Royal Institute of British Architects, in a volume entitled *The Story of Anne Whateley and William Shaxpere as Revealed by "The Sonnets to Mr. W. H." and Other Elizabethan Poetry* (1939). According to Ross, Anne was a nun residing at Temple Grafton near Stratford who "was a saint, had golden hair, and lived on a hill in country surroundings." Happening to meet the young "Shaxpere," come to the nunnery on business, Anne was immediately charmed, and she began to write sonnets to him. Eventually willing to sacrifice everything for her love of the Stratford lad, she left the nunnery, expecting to marry her admirer (a defection that explains her name being on the marriage register). In the meantime, though, Shakespeare, acting upon some well-known advice embodied in the sonnets, had met another Anne, Anne Hathaway. As the second Anne's claims upon him were more visible to the world, Shakespeare did the gentlemanly thing, and Anne Whateley, after a trip to Ireland to visit her old friend Spenser, returned to Temple Grafton and her sister nuns. It was there that she wrote the Shakespearean plays, plus a few other works of contemporary repute.

Ross extracts this story from the sonnets, first by changing certain masculine pronouns back to their original feminine form, and then by accepting the sonnet statements in what might be described as a hyper-literal manner. Some of his revelations are rather startling. Anne Hathaway, he tells us, was the dark lady, described by the poet/poetess as her "mistress" because "Shaxpere she worshiped with all the intensity of her being," and "spiritual marriage had sealed her oneness with him, therefore his wife was her 'mistress.'" She addressed the sonnets to a nonexistent Mr. W. H. merely for secrecy's sake (the "H" being, of course, the second letter in Shakespeare's name) and "many of the sonnets were sent or given to Shaxpere as explanations, answers, and love-letters as they were written." As a matter of fact, Ross informs us, "one or two, specially selected, may even have been read to Anne Hathaway as a gesture of friendship."

Anne Whateley, in a manner not made wholly clear, became the darling of every poet in Elizabethan England, and most of them admired her with something more than literary devotion, for "her would-be lovers were both ardent and numerous, and she, poor lady, sad at heart, hoping perhaps for a true response from one soul amongst them, reciprocated and encouraged her admirers." At the same time "her inmost self, however, remained inviolate," and even Michael Drayton gained "greatest favour" only "as a Platonic lover." An important result of this unprecedented charm was that many of the poets proceeded to celebrate Anne in their sonnet sequences, and while "it is not claimed

that all of the collections were inspired by Anne Whateley"
("a few were obviously written to other ladies"), it is
stressed that the fair nun was the inspiration for Barnabe
Barnes' *Parthenophe,* Giles Fletcher's *Licia,* Constable's
Diana, Daniel's *Delia,* and Drayton's *Idea,* among others.
Ross exhibits a certain scholarly restraint when dealing
with Sidney's sonnets, however, for he admits that "from
a perusal of these, it seems improbable that 'Stella' was
Anne Whateley."

Anne did, on the other hand, have a part in the composition of Sidney's work, writing pieces for him to claim as
his own, as she did for others in her circle of admirers.
Among her better-known efforts were the *Amoretti, Faërie
Queene,* and *Epithalamion,* the latter a poem that "celebrated 'imaginatively' the marriage of Anne Whateley and
Shakespeare." She wrote other works for her friend Spenser,
but, as Ross points out, "the work of differentiating fully
between the two poets is, however, beyond the reasonable
limits of this volume." She wrote also, *Hero and Leander,*
the "story of herself and William Shaxpere," and Marlowe's
plays, "preliminary efforts, written when she was acquiring
proficiency in the technique of the theatre." Thus the "invention of stage blank verse, hitherto attributed to Marlowe,
really belongs to Anne Whateley."

Anne's "full achievement as a creative artist was reserved
for Shaxpere alone," though, and "her offering to him was
the best of which her genius was capable." And it is a
pleasant change from the customary vilification of the
Stratford man to be told by Ross that Shakespeare was not
unappreciative of the glories accruing to his name, but attempted to repay the fair nun in kind with poems written
to Anne from his own hand. One, "Fidessa, more chaste
than kind" has wrongly been ascribed to "B. Griffin,
Gent."; another, to "Cynthia" (written after Anne's death
in 1600), was misappropriated by Sir Walter Raleigh. Both,

thanks to Ross, have now been returned to their rightful places in the true, if truncated, Shakespeare canon.

In 1950 William Ross's theory was revived, with modifications, by W. J. Fraser Hutcheson, a writer whose previous efforts had included a volume known as *Yesterday's Impossibilities,* and who was preparing, at the time, an anthology of Greek literature in modern rhyme to be entitled *Drops of Greece.* The Anne Whateley theory was set forth in *Shakespeare's Other Anne,* a book provocatively "Dedicated With Affection To The Ravens Around The Salt Tower." Actually, Hutcheson was not so much anti-Shakespeare as pro-Whateley, for the purpose of his book was "a swift and shallow skim over Elizabethan literature to reveal a very remarkable lady who nearly got William Shakespeare as a husband in 1582." Hutcheson's perfunctory acknowledgement that "we are indebted to Mr. William Ross, F.R.I.B.A., for some data from the Elizabethan sonneteers" hardly reveals how much of the "skim" is the result of Ross' previous researches.

Hutcheson's biographical discoveries (including the information that Anne was illegitimate) are inseparable from his literary revelations, for he claims for Anne the many Elizabethan poems signed "Ignoto," as well as other landmarks of Elizabethan writing, most of these works being annexed on the grounds that the common printing device ∴ was her own private symbol. As Hutcheson explains it:

She was a nun who masqueraded in print as a man, like Rosalind as Ganymede in 'As You Like It.' She was apparently the Touchstone who set the Elizabethan period ablaze with her own poetic talent, for she poured out prose and verse in prodigious quantity. She seems to have had command of very ample funds. She also sponsored, edited, assisted, and apparently financed several poets' publications and put her symbol on the title pages (∴), which symbol is the female glyph, the inverted triangle sign as old as the hills.

Among her more impressive literary accomplishments were most of Spenser's poems (e.g., the *Amoretti,* which "Spenser did not write all by himself, or we are poor sleuthhounds"), for "Ed. Sp. was more or less her stooge."

Hutcheson argues that "the hand of the poetess Anne Whateley is fairly apparent" in the Shakespearean sonnets, which is the excuse for discussing his theory here, if any is needed. His elaboration of Ross's picture of the Shakespeare-Hathaway-Whateley triangle is worth quoting.

We submit that the fair woman is Miss Whateley, the dark woman was Miss Hathaway, and the godlike Adonis is William *Hastas*haker. Of course, readers have been led astray by the switch of pronouns in seven or eight sonnets, and if the pronouns have their sex reversed, the puzzling content loses its tangle. . . . Miss Whateley was an English nun, sanctified, pure and chaste. None-the-less, we think William was a bit bored with it all in his young days. We are of the opinion, however, that he knew a good, sweet, wholesome and God-fearing woman when he met one, and he knew one in Anne Whateley the nun. . . . [The sonnets] ought to be read in their entirety, with the mind fairly assured that the principal author was a lady who loved, helped, guided, and collaborated with Shakespeare while she lived. . . . 'A Lover's Complaint' we take to be the nun's conception of the reactions of the dark woman, Hathaway, when she discovered that her junior Adonis, who had led her up the primrose path, had almost done the same thing, and with the same ease and technique, to a sacred nun; meaning Miss Anne Whateley, which notion is richly expressed in verse 38 thus:

My parts had power to charm a sacred nun,

. . . .

. . . Ah well, the dearly beloved nun died early in 1600/1. From that year onwards, Shakespeare gradually lost his jollity; he once overflowed with it. His mirth became morose. . . . Perhaps he had dieted too much on the Mr. W. H. Sonnets, and nurtured immutable regrets. It is not improbable that the jealous farmgirl Anne Hathaway expressed herself in some such rustic phrase as 'Good riddance to bad rubbish!' when the nun's lingering life expired, and thus further qualified for that notorious second-best bed.

Shakespeare's Other Anne ends with a series of appendices, the most intriguing of which lists the Elizabethan writers to whom the nun lent her glyph (˙·˙).

Seen in its true historical perspective, the theory that Calvin Hoffman of Long Island claims to have evolved hardly seems to rate the attention recently paid it in the newspapers and popular magazines. Hoffman argues that Christopher Marlowe (a university man, if not an aristocrat) wrote the plays, a thesis presented with some vigor in *The Murder of the Man Who Was 'Shakespeare'* (1955). He says that he was first led to suspect that Marlowe and Shakespeare might be the same man by noting various similarities of ideas and expression between the two, and his book contains a goodly number of these provocative parallels, some of the more revealing of which are given below.

MARLOWE	SHAKESPEARE
Edward II:	Richard II:
Bishop: My lord—	Northumberland: My lord—
King Edward: Call me not lord; away—out of my sight!	Richard: No lord of thine, thou haught, insulting man.
Dido, Queen of Carthage:	Macbeth:
Did ever men see such a sudden storm, Or day so clear so suddenly o'ercast?	So foul and fair a day I have not seen.
Hero and Leander:	Epitaph (on William Shakespeare's grave at Stratford, said to have been written by William Shakespeare):
Gentle youth, forbear To touch the sacred garments which I wear.	Good friend, for Jesus' sake forbear To dig the dust enclosed here.

Edward II:
Shape we our course to Ireland, there to breathe.

Richard II:
. . . To-morrow next
We will for Ireland; and 'tis time, I trow.

Edward II:
I arrest you of high treason.

Henry VIII:
I arrest thee of high treason.

Tamburlaine:
Blush, blush, fair city.

Macbeth:
Bleed, bleed, poor country.

Tamburlaine:
Fall, stars, that govern his nativity . . .

King Lear:
My nativity was under Ursa Major.

Tamburlaine:
Ah, cruel brat, sprung from a tyrant's loins!

Romeo and Juliet:
O serpent heart, hid with a flowering face!

Massacre of Paris:
. . . breakers of the peace!

Romeo and Juliet:
. . . disturbers of the peace!

Tamburlaine:
Here is my dagger.

Julius Caesar:
. . . there is my dagger.

Hoffman's parallels are not always as convincing as these, it must be admitted. One is dubious (detecting, indeed, a noticeable lack of scholarly restraint) when asked to believe that Shakespeare's "O, tiger's heart, wrapped in a woman's hide!" is paralleled in all three of the following passages from Marlowe: "Ah, cruel brat, sprung from a tyrant's loins!" "Inhuman creatures!—nursed with Tiger's milk," and "O Serpent that came creeping from the shore!" But citations of this latter sort represent only occasional enthusiasms; for the most part the parallels are similar in nature to those listed above.

Once Hoffman's keen ear (or eye?) had caught these striking similarities, his mind leapt to the natural conclusion that the so-called Shakespearean and Marlovian writings had to be the work of the same man. Not one easily intimidated by historical evidence, he decided that The Poet must be not Shakespeare (reported to have died in 1616), but Marlowe (reported to have been killed in a tavern brawl in 1593). The manner in which Hoffman o'erleaps the seemingly insurmountable obstacle of the plays' having been written after 1593 (for he accepts the orthodox dating) makes a tale not unworthy of Ross or Hutcheson. Perhaps it is best summarized in the words of a review appearing in the *Times Literary Supplement,* for the following paragraph gained a kind of official imprint from being about the only thing in the review to which Hoffman did not object.

[Finding himself in serious trouble with Elizabethan authorities] Christopher Marlowe jumped his bail on May 29, 1593, disguised himself, packed his Holinshed, his Halle, his Ovid, Seneca and Virgil, and took horse to Dover to cross the Channel. Next day, Robert Poley, Ingram Frizer and Nicholas Skeres murdered an unknown sailor. The sailor was buried on June 1, under the name of Marlowe. There was no inquest, for "Coroner Danby," bribed by Thomas Walsingham, returned a faked report. Marlowe, on the Continent, probably in Italy, sent back to Walsingham (with whom he had a homosexual relationship: Marlowe was "Walsingham's atheist lover") a number of writings, which were copied—probably by a scrivener named Thomas Smith, to whom Walsingham, in his will, left forty shillings. A "tight-lipped actor," William Shakespeare, "a steady, not too imaginative fellow," was bribed to give his name to the writings. Of the "36 plays, 154 sonnets, and two epic poems" which now go under the tight-lipped actor's name, the epic poem *Venus and Adonis* was already in the printer's hands; the rest were sent from abroad to Walsingham. Walsingham saw to the publication of the 1623 "Shakespeare" Folio and the manuscripts, back from the printer, may well have been buried, in 1630, with Walsingham in his tomb in Chislehurst Church in Kent.

Thus, the notorious brawl culminating in the murder of Marlowe, and seemingly attested to by contemporary police records, never occurred. The whole episode was merely a little drama (unfortunate, of course, for the sailor whose life was sacrificed that Marlowe might live) staged by Marlowe's lover, Sir Thomas Walsingham.

For one to whom the names of Delia Bacon, Dr. Owen, Roderick Eagle, and Maria Bauer are familiar, it will come as no surprise that Calvin Hoffman wanted the ocular proof, longing with traditional necrophilic fervor to force Sir Thomas' tomb in order to discover the "documentary evidence attesting to Christopher Marlowe's authorship of the plays and poems attributed to William Shakespeare." Of intense determination (he admits that "for almost two decades I pursued a literary will-o'-the-wisp that gave me no rest"), Hoffman actually did receive permission to open Walsingham's tomb in Kent. The thought of what he was about to undertake must have been sobering (did he recall the tragic indecision of Delia Bacon?), for he prepared himself against the dangers of sudden disappointment by a bit of stoic shoulder-squaring, published in the *New York Herald Tribune*.

And if what I seek is *not* found in the tomb? Will my postulate be voided forthwith? Not a whit! It will merely eliminate one possibility. Others exist. Each, in turn, will be investigated. Come what may, my basic thesis will hold as strong, and rock-firm, as ever.

As "Marlowe" said, "ripeness is all!" And so, armed with an exclusive contract to report his findings in the pages of the *Tribune,* Hoffman sailed for England in the spring of 1956, encouraged by the good wishes of a host of excited mystery addicts, including, he confided to the British press, "Mr. Hoover, the former president." What ensued is reported in the good, gray words of the London *Times.*

The theory that Christopher Marlowe was the real author of plays attributed to William Shakespeare encountered a setback at St. Nicholas's Church, Chislehurst, Kent, yesterday, when the Walsingham tomb in the Scadbury chapel was prised open and found to contain nothing but sand.

To the waiting world it was clear that when Hoffman had written, "will Walsingham's tomb reveal a manuscript which will read: The Tragedie of Hamlet, Prince of Den-mark by Christopher Marlowe?" he had put the cart before the horse. The question he first must answer is "Where is Sir Thomas?"

Calvin Hoffman claims that "it was not until at least 12 years had elapsed in my research" that he learned of Marlowe's name having previously occurred in discussions of the Shakespearean authorship. Actually, the Marlowe theory is one of the oldest in the long history of the controversy, having been advanced in 1895 by a San Francisco attorney, Wilbur Gleason Zeigler. According to Zeigler, Marlowe was not killed in the notorious brawl, but instead killed his adversary, who by a happy chance resembled Marlowe so closely that he could be dressed in the poet's clothes and buried in his name. Marlowe then went into hiding, where he wrote the plays that he allowed Shakespeare to dispose of as his own.

Zeigler's theory is presented in the form of a novel en-titled *It Was Marlowe. A Story of the Secret of Three Centuries,* but in spite of his using the technique of fiction, the author is completely serious about his claims, going so far as to include an argumentative preface and appendix to support his case. Hoffman's only acknowledgment of Zeigler's strikingly similar hypothesis comes in what might be described as a prudential footnote, where he admits that Zeigler "in a cinematic 'thriller,' fictionalized the tale of Marlowe's 'murder' by *reversing,* of all things, the docu-mented facts." In view of the closeness of Zeigler's narrative to his own story, Hoffman's charge that "the whole tale is compounded of the purest fiction and fantasy" seems un-wise. Perhaps it would have been more scholarly to have ad-mitted that the main purpose of Zeigler's book was to show

that Marlowe was "Shakespeare," a point that Hoffman
studiously avoids mentioning.

The Marlowe theory received support in 1901 from Dr.
T. C. Mendenhall in an article entitled "A Mechanical Solution of a Literary Problem." Writing in *Popular Science
Monthly,* Dr. Mendenhall told how he had worked out
a method of analyzing graphically the length of the words
employed by various writers. With the help of Mrs. Richard Mitchell and Miss Amy C. Whitman of Worcester,
Massachusetts, the doctor analyzed the "literature of the
Shakespearean period," where "in the counting and plot-
ting of the plays of Christopher Marlowe . . . something
akin to a sensation was produced among those actually engaged in the work." The sensation was that "in the characteristic curve of his plays Christopher Marlowe agrees
with Shakespeare about as well as Shakespeare agrees with
himself."

With commendable caution Dr. Mendenhall admitted
that his method could "never do more than direct inquiry
or suspicion." Similar restraint was demonstrated by Henry
Watterson, who in 1920 admitted in *Reedy's Mirror* that
"my own guess—we can only guess—has always been that
Christopher Marlowe wrote the plays." More positive was
Archie Webster, writing for the *National Review* in 1923.
"Was Marlowe the Man?" is described by Hoffman, in another footnote, as "a terse six-page magazine piece" advo-
cating Marlowe as the author of the sonnets. Hoffman fails
to reveal that Webster develops more than just the theory
that Marlowe wrote the sonnets, arguing that the poet did
not die in the controversial brawl but survived it and lived
out his life in exile. Webster concludes: "my examination
of the plays and their histories reveals much evidence that
Marlowe wrote all of the immortal plays that we are accustomed to speak of as 'truly Shakespearean.' " It is obvi-

ous that Calvin Hoffman is guilty of serious omissions in the matter of acknowledging his indebtedness to previous writers. Whatever inspired these omissions, they do not incline the reader to confidence in Hoffman's current historical revelations; nor in his future labors, even though rumor has it that he is to employ an electronic brain in his efforts to prove his case.

With Calvin Hoffman, our survey is almost complete, there remaining only a brief discussion in its historical context of George Elliott Sweet's *Shake-speare The Mystery* to finish the story. In the light of what the reader now knows about the Shakespeare controversy, it might not be inappropriate to begin with a glance at Mr. Sweet's qualifications for literary research, for according to the dust jacket of *Shake-speare The Mystery,* "no other student of the mystery of Shake-speare has the solid background for scientific investigation as has the author." Included in this background are the presidency of "Blue Pencil" (a high school literary fraternity), a B.S. in Chemistry, a "Master's" in Physics, and command of the Boston Magnetic Ranges during the last war (when Sweet was a lieutenant in the Naval Reserve). In addition, Mr. Sweet is president of the Sweet Geophysical Company, and, significantly, married to a lawyer. His further qualifications include a retiring disposition which, coupled with the opportunity for extensive travel, has led him to visit many libraries. But, for all his retiring disposition, "there is no library from New York to California which he has had an opportunity to enter that has not seen his face." Some idea of the extent of his research can be gathered from the statement that "libraries in such towns as Amarillo, Dallas, Houston, Oklahoma City, Bartlesville, Mobile, Yuma, and countless others have had their store of books covering the Elizabethan age examined."

The method by which it is determined that Queen Eliza-

beth was the author of the Shakespearean works consti-
tutes what Sweet terms "a scientific approach." He begins
by "dethroning" William Shakespeare and then proceeds
to look for that contemporary of the Stratford man who
best fits the personality of the plays and and poems. Shakespeare is eliminated on the scientific grounds that had he
written the various works that comprise the canon, he
would have ridden "a literary rocket at supersonic speed
to stratospheric fame," a journey manifestly impossible for
a mere actor, a minor one at that.

The true author, Mr. Sweet maintains, will be able to
pass the " 'universal-genius' test" and the " 'myriad-minded'
test," obstacles that quickly eliminate most of the literary
figures of Shakespeare's day. For example, when Sweet
compared "Shake-speare" and Francis Bacon, he realized
that "the two genii were poles apart in their thinking."
Furthermore, the author must have "Negative capability,"
that Keatsian ability of "being in uncertainties, mysteries,
doubts, without any irritable reaching after fact and reason." As Sweet points out, Queen Elizabeth, with her
known fondness for *laissez faire* in all fields of princely en-
deavor, fits this last requirement perfectly—was indeed a
veritable "Doctor of the Philosophy of Negative Capability." In addition, she was "myriad-minded" and by the
acclamation of the age a "universal-genius." She was also a
great admirer of Horace, who had written that "Five acts
a play must have, nor more nor less, / To keep the stage
and have a marked success," and it is most significant, in
Sweet's opinion, that "every one of Shake-speare's thirty-
seven plays has five acts, 'nor more, nor less.' "

Sweet discusses in some detail Elizabeth's role in the deception. He describes the three vows mentioned at the beginning of this account: the first to celibacy; the second of
marriage to England; the third to literature. He admits that
"history does not record either the vow to celibacy at fifteen

or the vow to literature at forty-five, yet the thoughtful historian will recognize the plausibility of both vows." Thus, "Elizabeth must be placed far ahead of the other candidates on the scale of probability."

Mr. Sweet rearranges the conventional chronology of the plays to fit Elizabeth's life span, explaining her failure to have any of the early works produced in the theater by her observance of Horace's advice to the young author to be slow in revealing early work to the world: "It is not illogical that Shake-speare [i.e., Elizabeth] followed the GOOD NINE YEARS KEEP IT SHUT CLOSELY UP IN YOUR SCRUTORE advice of Horace like he followed all the other precepts of Horace." He explains that the real Shake-speare, the Stratford actor, had no idea whose works he was assuming title to, Elizabeth choosing him only for the sensible reason that his name expressed her political philosophy of "talk softly and carry a big stick." Concerning the perplexing question of why such deception was necessary in the first place, Sweet writes, "if Mary Ann Evans Cross had good reason to write *Silas Marner* and *Mill on the Floss* as George Eliot . . . what could be more logical than for Elizabeth to let Shake-speare be her pen name . . . ?" Furthermore, Sweet believes, there is a good chance that Elizabeth's manuscripts, originally given to the "work-horse" of the conspirators, the Countess of Pembroke, may even now be resting in the Queen's tomb.

The "final clue" to the deception is to be found in the epilogue to *Henry VIII,* a play usually thought to have been composed about 1612–1613, but actually written in 1583 as Elizabeth's first attempt at dramatizing history. According to Sweet, the drama, though written early, was carefully designed to be the last play produced, the "dramatization of the history of her father, her mother, and her baby self" having been early seen by the Queen as a fitting finale to her unusual theatrical career. At first glance, however, the epilogue seems quite innocent.

> 'Tis ten to one this play can never please
> All that are here: some come to take their ease,
> And sleep an act or two; but those, we fear,
> We have frighted with our trumpets; so 'tis clear,
> They'll say 'tis naught: others, to hear the city
> Abused extremely, and to cry 'That's witty!'
> Which we have not done neither: that, I fear
> All the expected good we're like to hear
> For this play at this time, is only in
> The merciful construction of good women;
> For such a one we show'd 'em: if they smile,
> And say 'twill do, I know, within a while
> All the best men are ours: for 'tis ill hap
> If they hold when their ladies bid 'em clap.

But the lines are deceiving, for they actually contain the following valediction, unnoticed before the application of Sweet's "scientific approach."

'TIS TEN TO ONE
There are ten kings in Europe, I am the one queen.
             THIS PLAY CAN NEVER PLEASE
ALL THAT ARE HERE:
When I am disclosed to be Shake-speare, the announcement will displease many people
             SOME COME TO TAKE THEIR EASE,
AND SLEEP AN ACT OR TWO;
It may be one or two centuries before the riddle is solved.
             BUT THOSE, WE FEAR,
WE HAVE FRIGHTED WITH OUR TRUMPETS:
The disclosure will come as a shock to many people.
             SO 'TIS CLEAR
THEY'LL SAY 'TIS NAUGHT:
Many will say there is nothing in the theory.
             OTHERS TO HEAR THE CITY
ABUSED EXTREMELY, AND TO CRY 'THAT'S WITTY!'

*If the riddle is not solved for many years, this will be a great joke
on the literary men of London, especially if a foreigner resolves
the riddle.*

WHICH WE HAVE NOT DONE NEITHER:
*I have not planned this as a joke on London. I had good reason
for using the pseudonym Shake-speare. It should be realized that
the English people are too close to the English forest to spot the
significance of a single tree.*

THAT, I FEAR
ALL THE EXPECTED GOOD WE'RE LIKE TO HEAR
FROM THIS PLAY AT THIS TIME, IS ONLY IN THE
MERCIFUL CONSTRUCTION OF GOOD WOMEN:
*It will be the womenfolk who will have patience and understand-
ing with such a translation.*

FOR SUCH A ONE WE SHOW'D 'EM:
*I revealed myself in the body of the play. I was not in the Drama-
tis Personae. I did not speak, but I was SHOWN to the audience.*

IF THEY SMILE,
AND SAY 'TWILL DO, I KNOW, WITHIN A WHILE,
ALL THE BEST MEN ARE OURS; FOR 'TIS ILL HAP,
IF THEY HOLD WHEN THEIR LADIES BID 'EM CLAP.
*If the ladies approve this theory, then men will be brought to the
same point of view but it will take time. Some men will never be
convinced.*

Mr. Sweet's book is endorsed by Erle Stanley Gardner,
who contributes a preface in which Sweet is described both
as having "the mark of a great writer" and as being "one
of the outstanding literary detectives of the day." Gardner
further compliments Sweet on his "interesting body of
proof" and the manner in which it is handled; for "there is,
moreover, something so completely logical about the manner in which his mind moves from point to point, that one
realizes his presentation is indicative of remarkable skill in
collecting the facts, presenting them and thereafter drawing
a logical conclusion from them." In the face of this panegyric, it might not be amiss to remind the reader that Erle

Stanley Gardner is not only a writer of detective stories, but also a lawyer.

Shake-speare The Mystery is a far more original book than *The Murder of the Man Who Was 'Shakespeare';* nevertheless, it should be noted that the possibility of a Queen Elizabeth theory had occurred to writers prior to Mr. Sweet. In fact, one could argue that it was inevitable after 1910, the year Bram Stoker made the startling proposition that Queen Elizabeth was actually a man, in his book, *Famous Impostors.* In 1913, the reader will recall, J. M. Robertson predicted the appearance of the theory; in the same year W. R. Titterton actually claimed that Queen Elizabeth was the author, although his arguments in *New Witness* were obviously not meant to be taken too seriously. But Sweet's book is the first detailed presentation of Elizabeth Tudor's claims, and as such its literary importance is too obvious to require comment.

EPILOGUE

Our revels now are ended, and perhaps the author, like Prospero, may be allowed to reflect upon them for a moment. As they melt into history, the actors of our pageant leave certain ineradicable impressions behind. First, is a sense of their sincerity—with very few exceptions, the people whose writings are here chronicled have been honestly convinced that Shakespeare did not deserve his fame, and that, as a corollary, their own candidate had been robbed of the glory rightfully his. Equally strong is the impression of militant idealism— the idea of the Poet is very clear to them and very important, and they resist bitterly any invasion of that splendid concept. Closely related to the ideal, is the sensitive class-consciousness shared by all dissenters, who are attracted to Ariel and repelled by Caliban, overlooking the fact that to Caliban the author of *The Tempest* has given some of the loveliest lines in the play. Finally, they are all, no matter how much disguised by the trappings of historical scholarship, romantics at heart, romantics of an older, richer, more Keatsian school, enamored of cloud-capped towers and gorgeous palaces, of handsome knights and lovely ladies.

It is not surprising, therefore, that certain features are common to any argument that Shakespeare did not write the plays. Inevitably, the negative case is based upon those known facts of Shakespeare's life that reveal him to have been an ordinary lower-middle-class person, possessor of all those plebeian virtues which in a poet are embarrassing, but in a people the cause of national boasting. But then it is easier, one must admit, to argue on the basis of character and environment that a man *could not* have done something, than it is to go out and find actual proof that he *did not*. Similarly, the positive case is always presented in terms of probabilities, not of actualities; and, as we have seen, without the check of factual evidence some very complex historical theories are possible. Inevitably the result is the substitution of a series of involved hypotheses in place of a disappointingly small number of historical facts.

The question is frequently asked, if, when all is said and done, it matters who actually did write the plays and poems; and the question is deserving of an answer. Whether it matters to William Shakespeare, I do not know. That it does matter, on purely emotional grounds, to a great many people who love the Shakespearean works, I do know. But the real significance of the battle over the authorship goes far beyond Shakespeare and the controversial literature, for it strikes at the heart of man's knowledge of himself. The reasons we have for believing that William Shakespeare of Stratford-on-Avon wrote the plays and poems are the same as the reasons we have for believing any other historical event—for believing that Julius Caesar was stabbed by Brutus and the conspirators, that Charles I lost his head, that Abraham Lincoln was shot watching a performance of *Our American Cousin*. We believe these things because, in the opinion of those best qualified to judge, the historical evidence says that they happened. In exactly the same way the historical evidence says that William Shakespeare wrote the plays and poems. If one can argue that the evidence in Shakespeare's case does not mean what it says, that it has been falsified to sustain a gigantic hoax that has remained undetected for centuries, then one can just as surely argue that other evidence is not to be trusted and that, as Henry Ford said, "history is bunk." That is why the charge that Shakespeare did not write the plays does matter. And that is why, until contradictory factual evidence is unearthed, there appears to be no valid reason to doubt that the official records, the evidence of title pages, the testimony of self-described friends and fellow writers, mean just what they appear to say—that William Shakespeare of Stratford was the author of the wonderful works that bear his name.

INDEX

(No entries have been made for Francis Bacon or for William Shakespeare. References to Bacon occur mainly in the first three chapters.)